REVISED EDITION

# Financial Statement Analysis

The Investor's Self-Study Guide to Interpreting & Analyzing Financial Statements

## Charles J. Woelfel

**IRWIN**
*Professional Publishing®*
Chicago • London • Singapore

This publication is designed to provide accurate and authoritative information in regard to the subject matter covered. It is sold with the understanding that the author and the publisher are not engaged in rendering legal, accounting, or other professional service.

ISBN 1-55738-532-7

Printed in the United States of America

BB

5 6 7 8 9 0

RR/BJS

*To Colette*

# *TABLE OF CONTENTS*

## Chapter 3

## Chapter 4

## Chapter 5

# INTRODUCTION

*Financial Statement Analysis* is all about using accounting information to make business and investment decisions. Financial statements are summaries of the extensive activities of a business. *Financial Statement Analysis* is designed for informed business persons, investors, and creditors who must understand how to read, interpret, and analyze financial statements. It focuses on techniques used by analysts, investors, managers, and others to evaluate the financial position, operating performance, and cash flows of a business. A major source of such information is the financial statement of a company.

Investors purchase stock with the expectation that they will receive dividends and an increase in the value of the stock with a relative degree of assurance that their investment will be secure. Creditors make loans with the expectation of receiving interest and a return of principal. Investors and creditors assume the risk that their expectations will not be attained. Financial statement analysis can help them predict the amount of expected returns and assess the risk associated with their investments and loans.

Managers and owners of businesses often use financial statement analysis to identify and assess major changes in trends, amounts, and relationships related to their company's operating, investing, and financing activities. Financial statement analysis is an organized approach for extracting relevant information from financial statements for making business decisions.

Financial statement analysis can enhance your chance for success in investing, lending, and decision making by providing the background, tools, and techniques that professionals use on a day-to-day basis. Realistic examples and illustrations of financial statement analysis are used throughout this book to make the subject matter crystal clear. This is the major objective of this book. The information presented in this book is indispensable for the successful investor, creditor, or business person. You will want to add this book to your personal and professional library.

*Financial Statement Analysis* explains the objectives and methods of financial analysis in a meaningful manner. The generally accepted accounting principles used in compiling financial statements and the qualitative characteristics of the information presented on the statements are thoroughly and authoritatively discussed. After a thorough overview of financial statements, the major tools and techniques associated with financial statement analysis are explained, including:

1. Horizontal and vertical analysis

2. Common-size statements

3. Financial ratios (interpretation and use; applications and limitations)

4. Liquidity, activity (efficiency), and profitability ratios

5. Capital structure and solvency ratios

The chapters on financial ratios include "Quick Self-Study" exercises and problems. Solutions are provided immediately after the exercises and problems for your convenience.

Because of its significance, a special chapter has been devoted to the analysis of the statement of cash flows. The statement of cash flows provides a summary of a company's use of cash and its cash-related operating, investing, and financing activities. How a company spends its cash today largely determines its sources of cash in the future.

The significance of interim financial statements and segment reporting also is explored, as are practices associated with coping with inflation and current value changes. Special situations which arise in the real world are discussed, including

1. Personal financial statements

2. Development-stage companies

3. Companies in financial distress

4. Business combinations (mergers, acquisitions, consolidations)

5. Foreign operations and transactions

6. Related party transactions

7. Fraudulent financial statements and reporting

The final chapter offers an extensive set of review problems with solutions that provide an opportunity for the reader to master many of the techniques presented in this book.

The analytical techniques discussed in this book are well within the limits of today's microcomputer technology. Once the concepts are understood, the computer can be used to eliminate much of the computational tedium involved.

The author wants to thank the many people involved in bringing this book to you, especially the administration and staff at Probus Publishing Company. My special thanks to my wife, Colette, without whose patient perseverance and helpful counsel this book would not have been attempted or completed.

# Chapter 1

# OBJECTIVES OF FINANCIAL STATEMENT ANALYSIS AND FINANCIAL REPORTING

Financial statement analysis is a process that examines past and current financial data for the purpose of evaluating performance and estimating future risks and potentials. Financial statement analysis is used by investors, creditors, security analysts, bank lending officers, managers, governmental agencies, suppliers, and many other parties who rely on financial data for making economic decisions about a company. The emphasis of this book is on the needs of investors, especially shareholders and bondholders.

Analysis of financial statements focuses primarily on data provided in external reports plus supplementary information provided by management. The analysis should identify major changes or turning points in trends, amounts, and relationships. Financial statements are merely summaries of detailed financial information. Many different groups are interested in getting inside financial statements, especially investors and creditors. Their objectives are sometimes different but often related. However, the basic tools and techniques of financial statement analysis can be applied effectively by all of the interested groups. Financial statement analysis can assist investors in finding the type of information they require for making decisions relating to their interests in a particular company.

## INVESTOR'S NEEDS

Investors and potential investors are primarily interested in evaluating the investment characteristics of a company. Investment characteristics of an investment include such factors as risk, return, dividend or interest yield, safety, liquidity, growth, and others.

The relationship of the current value of a stock or bond to expectations of its future value is basically involved in the evaluation of investment opportunities. Investors are also interested in the safety of their investment as reflected in the financial condition of the company and its operating performance. The dividend policy of a company is usually a major concern of investors. Investors are also interested in the operating income of the firm in order to evaluate the normal earnings trend of the firm. Since many investors are interested in growth potential, they look for information concerning how the company obtained its resources and how it uses them. What is the capital structure of the company? What risks and rewards does it hold out for equity investors? Does the firm have any financial leverage? Investment evaluation also involves predicting the timing, amounts, and uncertainties of future cash flows of the firm.

Investors are also interested in monitoring the activities and effectiveness of management. Information about how management acquires resources and uses the resources under its control can influence investment decisions. The track record of management is often the most critical factor in deciding whether or not to invest in the securities of a particular firm.

Bondholders and other creditors of the company are primarily concerned with the company's ability to meet its obligations. Lenders want to know the reasons for a company's borrowings. Are they short- or long-term needs? Are they self-liquidating? How has the company handled its debt in the past?

Investment analysts and financial advisors have a major interest in the tools and techniques of financial statement analysis. Such persons have the same basic information needs as investors and creditors as it relates to their clients and potential clients. Analysts frequently adjust the financial statements prepared by accountants for items they do not consider significant or for items they consider significant but that do not appear on the statements.

## OBJECTIVES OF FINANCIAL REPORTING

Financial reporting provides information that is useful in making business and economic decisions. The objectives of general purpose external financial reporting come primarily from the needs of external users who must rely on information that management communicates to them.

The Financial Accounting Standards Board, in its conceptual framework of accounting project, identified the major objectives of financial reporting. These objectives can be summarized as follows:

1. Financial reporting should provide information that is useful to present and potential investors and creditors and other users in making rational investment, credit, and similar decisions. The information should be comprehensive to those who have a reasonable understanding of business and economic activities and are willing to study the information with reasonable diligence.

2. Financial reporting should provide information to help present and potential investors and creditors and other users in assessing the amounts, timing, and uncertainty of prospective cash receipts from dividends or interest and the proceeds from the sale, redemption, or maturity of securities or loans. Since investors' and creditors' cash flows are related to enterprise cash flows, financial reporting should provide information to help investors, creditors, and others assess the amounts, timing, and uncertainty of prospective net cash inflows to the related enterprise.

3. Financial reporting should provide information about the economic resources of an enterprise, the claims to those resources (obligations of the enterprise to transfer resources to other entities and owners' equity), and the effects of transactions, events, and circumstances that change its resources and claims to those resources.

The primary focus of financial reporting is ordinarily considered to be information about earnings and its components. Earnings analysis gives clues to (a) management's performance, (b) long-term earning capabilities, (c) future earnings, and (d) risks associated with lending to and investing in the enterprise.

Financial reporting should also provide information about how management has discharged its stewardship function to stockholders for the use of the enterprise's resources entrusted to it. Management is responsible not only for the custody and safekeeping of enterprise resources but also for their efficient and profitable use.

Management through financial reporting can provide significant financial information to users by identifying events and circumstances and explaining their financial effects on the enterprise. However, investors, creditors, and others who rely on financial reporting must do their own evaluating, estimating, predicting, and assessing and not rely exclusively on management's presentations.

## QUALITATIVE CHARACTERISTICS OF ACCOUNTING INFORMATION

Qualitative characteristics of accounting information are those qualities or ingredients of accounting information that make it useful. The Financial Accounting Standards Board has identified the basic qualitative characteristics that make accounting information useful and that are the qualities to be sought when accounting choices are made. The diagram in Exhibit 1.1 outlines a hierarchy of accounting information qualities. Exhibit 1.2 provides a summary of definitions used in Exhibit 1.1.

The hierarchical arrangement in Exhibit 1.1 is used to show certain relationships among the qualities. The hierarchy shows that information useful for decision making is the most important. The primary qualities are that accounting information shall be relevant and reliable. If either of these two qualities is completely missing, the information cannot be useful. To be relevant, information must be timely, and it must have predictive value, feedback value, or both. To be reliable, information must have representational faithfulness, and it must be verifiable and neutral. Comparability, including consistency, is a secondary quality that interacts with relevance and reliability and contributes to the overall usefulness of information. Two constraints are shown on the chart in Exhibit 1.1: (1) benefits must exceed costs and (2) materiality. To be useful and worth providing, the benefits of information should exceed its cost. All of the qualities described are subject to a materiality threshold. The hierarchy of qualitative characteristics does not rank the characteristics. If information is to be useful, all characteristics are required to a minimum degree. At times various qualities may conflict in particular circumstances, in which event trade-offs are often necessary or appropriate. For example, the most relevant information may be difficult to understand, or information that is easy to understand may not be very relevant.

## ELEMENTS OF FINANCIAL STATEMENTS

Elements of financial statements are the building blocks with which financial statements are constructed—the classes of items that financial statements comprise. The items in financial statements represent in words and numbers certain entity resources, claims to those resources, and the effects of transactions and other events and circumstances that result in changes in those resources and claims. Elements of financial statements defined in the FASB's *Statement of Financial Accounting Concepts No. 6*, "Elements of Financial Statements," include the following:

# Exhibit 1.1

## Qualitative Characteristics of Accounting Information

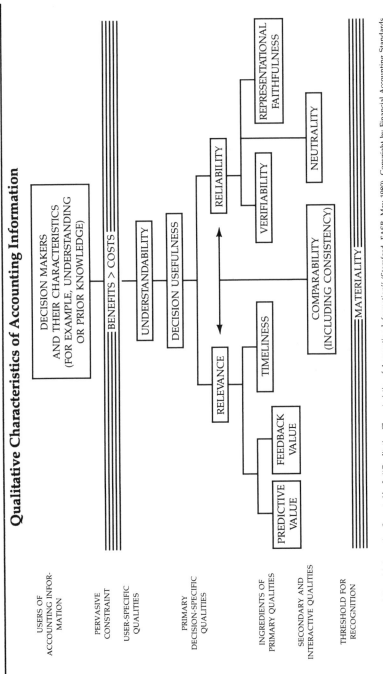

Source: *Statement of Financial Accounting Concepts No. 2*, "Qualitative Characteristics of Accounting Information" (Stamford, FASB, May 1980). Copyright by Financial Accounting Standards Board, High Ridge Park, Stamford, Connecticut 06905, U.S.A. Reprinted with permission.

## Exhibit 1.2

## Definitions: Qualitative Characteristics of Accounting Information

**Bias** Bias in measurement is the tendency of a measure to fall more often on one side than the other of what it represents instead of being equally likely to fall on either side. Bias in accounting measures means a tendency to be consistently too high or too low.

**Comparability** The quality of information that enables users to identify similarities in and differences between two sets of economic phenomena.

**Completeness** The inclusion in reported information of everything material that is necessary for faithful representation of the relevant phenomena.

**Conservatism** A prudent reaction to uncertainty to try to ensure that uncertainty and risks inherent in business situations are adequately considered.

**Consistency** Conformity from period to period with unchanging policies and procedures.

**Feedback Value** The quality of information that enables users to confirm or correct prior expectations.

**Materiality** The magnitude of an omission or misstatement of accounting information that, in the light of surrounding circumstances, makes it probable that the judgment of a reasonable person relying on the information would have been changed or influenced by the omission or misstatement.

**Neutrality** Absence in reported information of bias intended to attain a predetermined result or to induce a particular mode of behavior.

**Predictive Value** The quality of information that helps users to increase the likelihood of correctly forecasting the outcome of past or present events.

**Relevance** The capacity of information to make a difference in a decision by helping users to form predictions about the outcomes of past, present, and future events or to confirm or correct prior expectations.

**Reliability** The quality of information that assures that information is reasonably free from error and bias and faithfully represents what it purports to represent.

**Representational Faithfulness** Correspondence or agreement between a measure or description and the phenomenon that it purports to represent (sometimes called validity).

**Timeliness** Having information available to a decision maker before it loses its capacity to influence decisions.

**Understandability** The quality of information that enables users to perceive its significance.

**Verifiability** The ability through consensus among measures to ensure that information represents what it purports to represent or that the chosen method of measurement has been used without error or bias.

Source: *Statement of Financial Accounting Concepts No. 2.* "Qualitative Characteristics of Accounting Information" (Stamford, FASB, May 1980).Copyright © by Financial Accounting Standards Board, High Ridge Park, Stamford, Connecticut 06905, U.S.A. Reprinted with permission.

1. *Assets* are probable future economic benefits obtained or controlled by a particular entity as a result of past transactions or events.

2. *Liabilities* are probable future sacrifices of economic benefits arising from present obligations of a particular entity to transfer assets or provide services to other entities in the future as a result of past transactions or events.

3. *Equity* or net assets is the residual interest in the assets of an entity that remain after deducting its liabilities. In a business enterprise, the equity is the ownership interest.

4. *Investment by owners* are increases in equity of a particular business enterprise resulting from transfers to it from other entities of something valuable to obtain or increase ownership interests (or equity) in it.

5. *Distributions to owners* are decreases in equity of a particular business enterprise resulting from transferring assets, rendering services, or incurring liabilities by the enterprise to owners. Distributions to owners decrease ownership interest (or equity) in an enterprise.

6. *Comprehensive income* is the change in equity of a business enterprise during a period from transactions and other events and circumstances from nonowner sources. It includes all changes in equity during a period except those resulting from investments by owners and distributions to owners.

7. *Revenues* are inflows or other enhancements of assets of an entity or settlements of its liabilities (or a combination of both) from delivering or producing goods, rendering services, or other activities that constitute the entity's ongoing major or central operations.

8. *Expenses* are outflows (or other using up of assets or incurrences of liabilities or a combination of both) from delivering or producing goods, rendering services, or carrying out other activities that constitute the entity's ongoing major or central operations.

9. *Gains* are increases in equity (net assets) from peripheral or incidental transactions of an entity and from all other transactions and other events and circumstances affecting the entity except those that result from revenues or investments by owners.

10. *Losses* are decreases in equity (net assets) from peripheral or incidental transactions of an entity and from all other transactions and other events and circumstances affecting the entity except those that result from expenses or distributions to owners.

## SUMMARY

Financial statement analysis is not an end in itself but is performed for the purpose of providing information that is useful in making lending and investing decisions. An understanding of analytical methods associated with financial statement analysis is extremely useful when interpreting and analyzing financial reports.

The objectives of financial reporting are designed to meet the needs of investors and creditors for decision making purposes. The primary focus of financial reporting is information about earnings and its components. Information useful in evaluating the amounts, timing, and uncertainty of prospective cash receipts from dividends or interest and the proceeds from the sale, redemption, or maturity of securities or loans is basic to many investment decisions. These and other concerns are the basic objectives of financial reporting.

The qualitative characteristics of accounting information are those qualities that enhance its usefulness for decision making. Relevance and reliability are the two primary qualities that make accounting information useful for decision making. Predictive value, feedback value, and timeliness are the three components of relevance. Representational faithfulness and verifiability are the components of reliability. The qualitative characteristics of useful accounting information are pervasive and provide a basis for choosing among accounting and reporting alternatives.

# Chapter 2

# ACCOUNTING ASSUMPTIONS, PRINCIPLES, PROCEDURES, AND POLICIES

An understanding of the assumptions, principles, procedures, and policies underlying financial statements will be helpful in understanding the nature and scope of financial statement analysis. In this chapter, accounting assumptions, principles, procedures, and policies will be discussed.

## ACCOUNTING ASSUMPTIONS

**Accounting assumptions** are broad concepts that underlie generally accepted accounting principles and serve as a foundation for these principles. The major accounting assumptions include the following: the business entity assumption, the continuity assumption, the periodic and timely reporting assumption, and the monetary unit assumption.

The most basic accounting assumption is that economic activity can be identified with a particular unit or entity of accountability. The unit or entity to be accounted for can be defined as an area of economic interest to a particular individual or group. Corporations, sole proprietorships, and partnerships are examples of accounting entities. The **business entity assumption** determines the nature and scope of the reporting that is required for the unit or entity.

Accounting is based on the assumption that the accounting unit or entity is engaged in continuous and ongoing activities. The accounting unit or entity is assumed to remain in operation into the foreseeable future to achieve its goals and objectives. This assumption is referred to as the **continuity** or **going-concern assumption.** If evidence indicates that the unit or entity has a limited life, modifications in accounting principles, methods, and reporting practices would ordinarily be required; for example, in cases where corporate reorganization or liquidation under bankruptcy is involved.

The continuous operations of a business or other economic unit or entity over an extended period of time can be meaningfully segmented into equal time periods, such as a year, quarter, or month. The **periodic and timely reporting assumption** requires that accounting reporting should be done periodically and on a timely basis so that it is relevant and reliable.

The **monetary unit assumption** requires that financial information be measured and accounted for in the basic monetary unit of the country in which the enterprise is located (dollars for U.S. firms). The monetary value of an economic event or transaction, determined at the time it is recorded, is not adjusted for subsequent changes in the purchasing power of the monetary unit.

## ACCOUNTING PRINCIPLES

**Accounting principles** are the guidelines, laws, or rules that are adopted by the accounting profession and that serve as guides to accounting practice. A major objective of accounting principles is to reduce the difference and inconsistencies in accounting practice, thereby improving the comparability and credibility of financial reports.

The phrase **generally accepted accounting principles,** or GAAP, is a technical term that identifies the accounting principles that represent accepted accounting practice at a particular period of time. GAAP reflect a consensus of what the accounting profession considers good accounting practices and procedures. GAAP establish which resources and obligations should be recorded as assets and liabilities, which changes in assets and liabilities should be recorded, when these changes should be recorded, how the recorded assets and liabilities and changes in them should be measured, what information should be disclosed, and which financial statements should be prepared. GAAP are prescribed by authoritative bodies such as the Financial Accounting Standards Board (FASB). The FASB's authoritative pronouncements are issued in the form of Statements of Financial Accounting Standards and Interpretations.

Major accounting principles include the historical (or acquisition) cost principle, the realization principle, the matching principle, the full disclo-

sure principle, the materiality principle, the conservatism principle, the consistency principle, and others.

The **historical (or acquisition) cost principle** states that the acquisition
cost is the proper amount at which transactions and events involving assets,
liabilities, and owners' equity should be initially recorded in the accounting
system. Transactions and events are measured by the exchange price at
which the transfer takes place. Cost is the exchange price in an arm's-length
transaction, that is, a transaction in which each of the parties involved is
seeking to serve his/her own best interest.

The **revenue realization principle** determines when revenue is to be considered realized. **Realization** refers to the process of converting noncash
resources and rights into money; the term is used in accounting and financial reporting to refer to sales of assets for cash or claims to cash. According
to the realization principle, revenue is realized when the sale takes place
because the earning process is substantially completed and an exchange has
taken place. It is also assumed that (1) the amount of revenue is determinable and its collection is reasonably assured, and (2) reasonable estimates
can be made of related future costs. Revenue from services rendered is
recognized when services have been performed and are billable. Revenue
from permitting others to use enterprise resources, such as interest, rent,
and royalties, is recognized as time passes or as the resources are used.
Exceptions to the basic revenue principle provide for the recognition of
revenue under the following conditions:

1.  Recognition when the sale price is collected, i.e., the cash method
    and the installment method.

2.  Recognition when the production process is completed, but before
    the sale, i.e., the production method.

3.  Recognition proportionally over the performance of a long-term
    contract, i.e., the percentage-of-completion method.

4.  Recognition at the completion of a long-term contract, i.e., the com-
    pleted contract method.

5.  Recognition of profit from the sale only after the payments received
    equal the cost of the item sold, i.e., the cost recovery method.

The **matching principle** requires that revenues generated and expenses
incurred in earning those revenues be reported in the same income statement. In this way, sacrifices (expenses) are matched against benefits or ac-
complishments (revenues). It is through the matching process that net
income is determined. General guidelines for applying the matching principle include the following:

1.  Associating cause and effect—Some costs are recognized as expenses on the basis of a presumed direct association with specific revenues. For example, sales commission expense can be associated with the sales revenue of the period and should be reported on the income statement when the sales revenue is reported.

2.  Systematic and rational allocation—Where there is no cause-and-effect relationship between revenue and expenses, an attempt is made to associate costs in a systematic and rational manner with the products of the period affected. For example, depreciation expense for office equipment has no cause-and-effect relationship to revenue of the period; the cost of the equipment should be depreciated in a systematic and rational manner over the life of the asset.

3.  Immediate recognition—Costs that cannot be related to revenues by either of the two preceding processes are recognized as expenses of the current period. For example, the salary of the company's president should be given immediate recognition as an expense in the period in which it is incurred.

The **full (or adequate) disclosure principle** requires that information provided in financial statements be sufficiently complete to avoid misleading users of the reports by omitting significant facts of information. The full disclosure principle also refers to revealing information that would be useful in the decision-making processes of informed users. Full disclosure is required for the fair presentation of financial statements. Many disclosures are made in the body of the financial statements and in notes (footnotes), schedules, and supplementary reports, and in a summary of significant policies preceding the first note to financial statements.

**Materiality** refers to the magnitude or significance of something that would be of interest to an informed investor or creditor in making evaluations and decisions. The **materiality principle** requires that anything that is material to financial statements must be disclosed. An item is material for accounting purposes if the omission or misstatement of it, in light of surrounding circumstances, makes it probable that the judgment of a reasonable person relying on the information would have been changed or influenced by the omission or misstatement. Immaterial items that have little or no consequences to statement users can be handled as expediency, fairness, and professional judgment require.

**Conservatism** is a basic accounting principle that requires the reasonable anticipation of potential losses in recorded assets or in the settlement of liabilities at the time when financial statements are prepared. The principle of conservatism is sometimes expressed as follows: "Recognize all losses and anticipate no gains." A major purpose of the principle of conservatism is to assure that assets will not be overstated or liabilities understated.

**Consistency** refers to the reporting practices from year to year within an entity. The consistency principle requires that a particular accounting principle, method, or procedure, once adopted, not be changed from period to period. Should management determine that a particular accounting treatment is not appropriate and should be changed, generally accepted accounting principles require that the facts related to the change and its dollar effects be reported.

## *ACCOUNTING PROCEDURES AND POLICIES*

**Accounting procedures** are those rules and practices that are associated with the operations of an accounting system and that lead to the development of financial statements. Accounting procedures include the methods, practices, and techniques used to carry out accounting objectives and to implement accounting principles. For example, last-in, first-out (LIFO) and straight-line depreciation are examples of accounting for inventory and buildings. Accounting procedures can vary from company to company and from industry to industry. An accounting procedure should be selected in a given circumstance if its use reflects generally accepted accounting principles and if it is appropriate to record, process, and report the event or transaction.

Information about the **accounting policies** adopted by a reporting enterprise is essential for financial statement users and should be disclosed. Accounting principles and their method of application in the following areas are considered particularly important:

1.  A selection from existing alternatives (for example, inventory methods such as LIFO, FIFO, and average methods).

2.  Areas that are peculiar to a particular industry in which the company operates.

3.  Unusual and innovative applications of generally accepted accounting principles.

Significant accounting policies are usually disclosed as the initial note or as a summary preceding the notes to the financial statements.

# OTHER ACCOUNTING CONSIDERATIONS

Major bases of accounting include the accrual basis and cash basis. In **accrual accounting,** revenue and gains are recognized in the period when they are earned. Expenses and losses are recognized in the period they are incurred. Accrual accounting is concerned with the economic consequences of events and transactions instead of merely with cash receipts and cash payments. Under accrual accounting, net income does not necessarily reflect cash receipts and cash payments for a time period. Accrual accounting generally provides the best measure of earnings, earning power, managerial performance, and stewardship.

**Cash-basis accounting** recognizes only transactions involving actual cash receipts and disbursements occurring in a given period. Cash-basis accounting recognizes revenues and gains when cash is received and expenses and losses when cash is paid. No attempt is made to record unpaid bills or amounts owed to or by the entity. No attempt is made to match revenues and expenses to determine income. Cash-basis accounting is widely used by small businesses and for income-tax purposes.

The **economic substance** of a transaction is sometimes considered more significant than the **legal form** of the transaction for reporting purposes. For example, consolidated financial statements are usually considered more relevant than are the separate statements of members of the affiliated group. Consolidated financial statements do not represent the legal statements of any accounting entity. However, they do represent an accounting entity. Some leases that are legal leases are considered the purchase and sale of an asset for accounting purposes. In this case, the economic substance of the transaction supersedes the legal form of the transaction.

# DEVELOPMENT OF ACCOUNTING STANDARDS

Various organizations have influenced the development of generally accepted accounting principles. Among these are the American Institute of Certified Public Accountants (AICPA), the Financial Accounting Standards Board (FASB), and the Securities and Exchange Commission (SEC). The first two are private sector organizations; the SEC is a federal government agency.

The American Institute of Certified Public Accountants is the national organization of CPAs. The AICPA played a major role in the development of accounting standards from 1937 to 1973. In 1937, the AICPA created the Committee on Accounting Procedure (CAP), which issued a series of *Accounting Research Bulletins* with the purpose of standardizing accounting practices. In 1959, this committee was replaced by the Accounting Principles Board (APB). The APB continued the series of ARBs and began to publish a new set of pronouncements, referred to as *Opinions of the Accounting Principles Board*. In mid-1973, an independent private board, the Financial Accounting Standards Board (FASB), replaced the APB and assumed responsibility for the issuance of financial accounting standards. The FASB is currently the primary source for the determination of financial accounting standards.

The Financial Accounting Standards Board has seven members who serve full time and are paid for their services. FASB members are not required to be CPAs. An affirmative vote of five of the seven members is needed to approve a pronouncement. It issues *Statements of Financial Accounting Standards* (SFAS), which establish new or amend existing generally accepted accounting principles. It also issues *Interpretations* and *Statements of Financial Accounting Concepts*. In 1984, the FASB established an Emerging Issues Task Force (EITF), which tries to anticipate and resolve, on a timely basis, accounting problems that are associated with new types of transactions. The task force publishes *Minutes* of its deliberations. Today accountants rely on a mixture of ARBs, APB Opinions, SFAS Statements, and Minutes of the EITF for authoritative guidance in financial accounting and reporting.

The Financial Accounting Standards Board typically uses the following steps in its standard-setting process:

1. Identifies an accounting problem and places the problem on its agenda.

2. Appoints a task force of technical experts which conducts extensive research on the problem.

3. Issues a Discussion Memorandum, that summarizes the major issues and possible solutions and serves as the basis for public comment.

4. Conducts a public hearing at which it invites interested parties to present their views.

5. Issues an Exposure Draft, which is a proposed SFAS that is distributed for public comment.

6. Issues an SFAS after it has analyzed public responses to the Exposure Draft and voted to approve the standard.

The FASB adopts a neutral position toward the economic consequences of its standards. However, it has been difficult for the FASB to ignore the impact of external financial statements on the allocation of economic resources and the distribution of wealth.

The Financial Accounting Standards Advisory Council assists the FASB in setting priorities and establishing ad hoc task forces, evaluating performance, and reacting to proposed standards.

The Financial Accounting Foundation (FAF) is an independent entity whose board of trustees oversees the basic structure of the standard-setting process. The trustees appoint members to the FASB and to the FASB's advisory council. The FAF also obtains private contributions to fund the FASB's operations. The trustees are appointed by a panel of representatives from several national organizations whose members have a knowledge of and an interest in corporate financial reporting. These organizations include the American Institute of Certified Public Accountants, American Accounting Association (primarily accounting educators), National Institute of Accountants (primarily industrial accountants), Financial Executives Institute (primarily financial executives), Financial Analysts Federation (a national organization of financial analysts), Securities Industry Association, National Association of State Auditors, Comptrollers and Treasurers, and Government Finance Officers Association.

The Governmental Accounting Standards Board (GASB) was created in 1984 to develop accounting standards for governmental units such as state and local entities. GASB operates under the oversight of the Financial Accounting Foundation and the Governmental Advisory Council.

Exhibit 2.1 shows the current organization, primary activities, and related organizational units of the FASB.

The Securities and Exchange Commission was created by the Securities Exchange Act of 1934 as an independent federal agency to administer all federal security laws, which include those provided in both the 1933 and 1934 Acts as well as the Public Utility Holding Company Act of 1935, the Trust Indenture Act of 1939, the Investment Company Act of 1940, the Investment Advisor Act of 1940, and the Foreign Corrupt Practices Act of 1977. The SEC is composed of five commissioners appointed by the president. No more than three of the commissioners can be of the same political party.

The SEC has the legal authority to prescribe accounting principles and methods for firms whose shares are sold to the investing public on the stock exchanges. The law requires that such companies make reports to the SEC giving detailed information about their operations. The SEC has broad powers to require public disclosure in a fair and accurate manner in financial statements and to protect investors. The SEC observes the private rule-making bodies and has on occasion exercised its influence in the standard-setting process.

The SEC requires numerous reports to be filed with it. Major reports include the following:

1.  Regulation S-X. A report required under the 1933 Act when a company makes a public offering of its securities. It includes such information as the nature of the company's business, a description of the securities being registered, and audited financial statements.

2.  Form 10-K. An annual report that must be filed with the SEC within 90 days of a company's fiscal year-end.

3.  Form 8-K. A report used to describe any significant events that may affect the company (such as a major acquisition or a lawsuit), which must be filed within 15 days after a material event has occurred.

## Exhibit 2.1

### Financial Accounting Foundation Structure

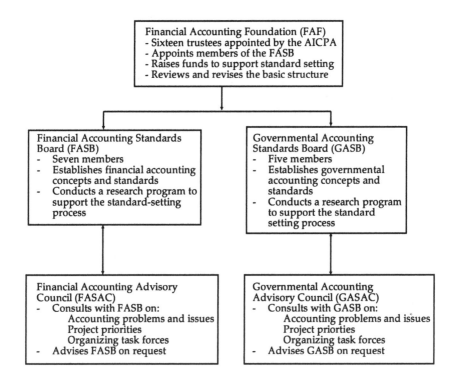

4. Proxy Statement. A report used when management requests the right to vote through proxies for shareholders at stockholders' meetings.

5. Form 10-Q. A quarterly report of operations that must be filed within 45 days of the end of each of the company's first three fiscal quarters.

The Internal Revenue Service prescribes rules, methods, and regulations for the determination of taxable income. These pronouncements can and do conflict at times with the accounting principles and methods acceptable for financial reporting. A company may keep more than one set of records to satisfy both reporting requirements.

## SUMMARY

Accounting assumptions provide the foundation for the structure of financial accounting theory and explain why financial information is presented in a given manner. Generally accepted accounting principles represent the standards and practices that a firm must use in preparing external financial statements. Generally accepted accounting principles or standards are prescribed by authoritative bodies, such as the Financial Accounting Standards Board, and are based on theoretical as well as practical considerations. These principles evolve and change in response to changes in the economic environment.

# Chapter 3

# *INSIDE FINANCIAL STATEMENTS*

Financial statements are the most widely used and most comprehensive way of communicating financial information about a business enterprise to users of the information provided on the reports. Different users of financial statements have different information needs. **General purpose financial statements** have been developed to meet the needs of users of financial statements, primarily the needs of investors and creditors.

The information provided by financial statements is primarily financial in nature, quantified and expressed in units of money. The information is summarized information and a subset of the total information needed by financial statement users. The information presented pertains to individual enterprises and not to industries or to members of society as a whole. The information is often provided on the statements in the form of approximations rather than exact measures. The measures involve estimates, classifications, summarizations, judgments, and allocations. The information generally reflects the financial effects of transactions and events that have already happened. The information provided involves a cost to provide and use; generally the benefits of information provided should be expected to at least equal the cost incurred in producing the information.

External financial statements prepared by companies are governed by two different authorities: The Financial Accounting Standards Board and regulatory authorities. The FASB's standards reflect generally accepted accounting principles. Regulators' accounting rules are commonly referred to as RAP. Statements prepared for general external distribution and for the Securities and Exchange Commission are required to use GAAP. Statements prepared for regulatory authorities must use RAP. Fortunately, many of the differences between GAAP and RAP are being reconciled.

The basic output of the financial accounting process is presented in the following interrelated general purpose financial statements:

1.  A **balance sheet** (or **statement of financial position**) summarizes the financial position of an accounting entity at a particular point in time.

2.  An **income statement** summarizes the results of operations for a given period of time.

3.  A **statement of cash flows** summarizes an enterprise's operating, financing, and investing activities as well as its cash receipts and disbursements over a given period of time.

4.  A **statement of retained earnings** shows the increases and decreases in earnings retained by the company over a given period of time.

**Notes** to financial statements are considered an integral part of financial statements. Notes provide additional information not included in the accounts on the financial statements. They are usually factual rather than interpretative. Notes should be read carefully and evaluated when financial statement analysis is undertaken.

The annual report of a company to its shareholders and others includes the four general purpose financial statements, supporting schedules, the auditor's report, historical financial highlights, and comments from management relating to the current fiscal year's activities. The financial statements included in the annual report are the responsibility of management and not of the auditor.

## CONSOLIDATED FINANCIAL STATEMENTS

Exhibits 3.1, 3.2, 3.4, and 3.5 present four consolidated financial statements for the Mythical Manufacturing Company. Footnotes and supplementary information applicable to the statements are not shown in the exhibits. **Consolidated financial statements** include a complete set of statements prepared for the consolidated entity and the sum of the assets, liabilities, revenues, and expenses of the affiliated companies after eliminating the effect of any transactions among the affiliated companies. Consolidated financial statements present the financial position and results of operations of the economic unit controlled by the parent company as a single accounting entity. Emphasis is placed on the economic unit under control of one management rather than on the legal form of the separate entities.

Consolidated financial statements are prepared primarily for the benefit of the shareholders and creditors of the parent company. There is a presumption that consolidated statements are more meaningful than the separate statements of members of the affiliation. However, subsidiary creditors, minority shareholders, and regulatory agencies must rely on the statements of the subsidiary to assess their claims. The usual condition for consolidating the statements of an affiliated group of companies is ownership of a majority voting interest in common stock. Ownership by one company, directly or indirectly, of over 50 percent of the outstanding voting shares of another company is required for consolidation.

## THE BALANCE SHEET

The **balance sheet** (or **statement of financial position**) is a report that shows the financial position of an enterprise at a particular time, including the firm's economic resources (assets), economic obligations (liabilities), and the residual claims of owners (owners' equity). Assets are usually shown in the order of their liquidity (nearness to cash) and liabilities in the order of their maturity date.

The balance sheet is usually presented in one of the following formats:

1.  Account form: Assets = Liabilities + Owners' equity
2.  Report form: Assets – Liabilities = Owners' equity

Major classifications used in the statement of financial position include the following:

1.  Assets:
    a.  Current assets (cash, marketable securities, accounts receivable, inventory, and prepaid expenses).
    b.  Investments.
    c.  Property, plant, and equipment.
    d.  Intangible assets (e.g., patents, copyrights, goodwill).
    e.  Deferred charges or other assets.
2.  Liabilities:
    a.  Current liabilities (accounts payable, notes payable, wages payable, accrued liabilities, unearned revenue).
    b.  Long-term liabilities.

3.   Owners' equity:

   a.   Capital stock.

   b.   Additional paid-in capital.

   c.   Retained earnings.

Balance sheets are usually presented in comparative form. Comparative statements include the current year's statement and statements of one or more preceding accounting periods. Comparative statements are useful in evaluating and analyzing trends and relationships. Exhibit 3.1 shows a comparative balance sheet for the Mythical Manufacturing Company.

### Exhibit 3.1

**Mythical Manufacturing Company Consolidated Balance Sheet December 31, 19X1 and 19X2 (thousands of dollars)**

**ASSETS**

|  | 19X2 | 19X1 |
|---|---|---|
| Current assets |  |  |
| Cash | $40,000 | $30,000 |
| Marketable securities—cost (market value 19X1 $88,000, 19X2 $69,000) | 80,000 | 64,000 |
| Accounts receivable—less allowance for doubtful accounts: 19X2 $5,000, 19X2 $4,500 | 312,000 | 290,000 |
| Inventories (LIFO cost) | 360,000 | 370,000 |
| Prepaid expenses | 8,000 | 6,000 |
| Total current assets | 800,000 | 760,000 |
| Property, plant, and equipment |  |  |
| Land | 60,000 | 60,000 |
| Buildings | 250,000 | 237,000 |
| Machinery | 430,000 | 372,200 |
| Office equipment | 30,000 | 24,000 |
| Total | 770,000 | 693,200 |
| Less accumulated depreciation | 250,000 | 195,000 |
| Total net property, plant, and equipment | 520,000 | 498,200 |
| Intangibles (patents, goodwill) | 4,000 | 5,000 |
| Total Assets | $1,324,000 | $1,263,200 |

## LIABILITIES

|  | 19X2 | 19X1 |
|---|---|---|
| Current liabilities |  |  |
| Accounts payable | $144,000 | $138,000 |
| Notes payable | 102,000 | 122,000 |
| Salaries payable | 60,000 | 72,000 |
| Income taxes payable | 34,000 | 30,000 |
| Total current liabilities | 340,000 | 362,000 |
| Long-term liabilities |  |  |
| Deferred income taxes | 20,000 | 18,000 |
| Bond payable 12.5% due 2020 | 272,000 | 272,000 |
| Total liabilities | $632,000 | $652,000 |

## STOCKHOLDERS' EQUITY

|  | 19X2 | 19X1 |
|---|---|---|
| Preferred stock $5.83 cumulative, |  |  |
| $100 par value, authorized 150,000 |  |  |
| outstanding 120,000 | $12,000 | $12,000 |
| Common stock $5 par value, |  |  |
| authorized 40,000,000 shares, |  |  |
| outstanding 19X2 30,000,000 shares, |  |  |
| 19X1 29,000,000 | 150,000 | 145,000 |
| Additional paid-in capital on common stock | 32,000 | 15,000 |
| Retained earnings |  |  |
| Unappropriated | 400,000 | 341,200 |
| Appropriated | 98,000 | 98,000 |
| Total stockholders' equity | 692,000 | 611,200 |
| Total liabilities and stockholders' equity | $1,324,000 | $1,263,200 |

**MEASUREMENTS USED IN FINANCIAL STATEMENTS.** Assets and liabilities reported on the balance sheet are measured by different attributes—for example, historical cost, current (or replacement) cost, current market value, net realizable value, and present value of future cash flows, depending on the nature of the item and the relevance and reliability of the attribute measured. **Historical cost** is the exchange price of the asset when it was acquired. **Current cost** is the amount of cash or its equivalent required to obtain the same asset at the balance sheet date. **Current market value** or exit value is the amount of cash that may be obtained at the balance sheet date from selling the asset in an orderly liquidation. **Net realizable value** is the amount of cash that can be obtained as a result of a future sale of an asset, less cost of disposing of the asset. **Present value** is the expected exit value discounted to the balance sheet date.

**ASSETS.** Assets are probable future economic benefits obtained or controlled by a particular entity as a result of past transactions or events. **Future economic benefits** refers to the capacity of an asset to benefit the enterprise by being exchanged for something else of value to the enterprise, by being used to produce something of value to the enterprise, or by being used to settle its liabilities. The future economic benefits of assets usually result in net cash inflows to the enterprise. Assets are recognized in the financial statements when (1) the item meets the definition of an asset, (2) it can be measured with sufficient reliability, (3) the information about it is capable of making a difference in user decisions, and (4) the information about the item is reliable.

**CURRENT ASSETS.** Current assets are cash and other assets that are expected to be converted into cash, sold, or consumed within the normal operating cycle of the business or one year, whichever is longer. An operating cycle is the average time required to expend cash for inventory, process and sell the inventory, collect the receivables, and convert the receivables into cash. Current assets include cash, marketable securities, accounts receivable, inventories, accrued revenues (assets), and prepaid expenses.

Cash represents money on hand and balances of checking accounts at banks. Cash includes coins, checks, money orders, bank drafts, and any item acceptable to a bank for deposit. A compensating balance arises when a bank lends funds to a customer and requires that a minimum balance be retained at all times in the customer's checking account. If compensating balances are not disclosed, misleading inferences about the company's liquidity and interest costs might be made.

**Marketable securities** include stocks, bonds, and similar securities that are to be converted into cash within the operating cycle of the business or within a year, whichever is longer, and that are readily marketable. Accounts usually report marketable securities at cost or at the lower of cost or market value.

**Accounts receivable** represent amounts due from customers arising from sales or from services performed. The **allowance for doubtful accounts** shown on most balance sheets is a contra-asset account. The allowance represents a reduction of the accounts receivable that is established to adjust this item to an estimate of the amount realizable. **Notes receivable**

are unconditional promises in writing to pay definite sums of money at certain or determinable dates, usually with a specified interest rate.

**Inventories** represent merchandise, work in process, and raw materials that a business normally uses in its manufacturing and selling operations. Inventories are usually reported at cost or at the lower of cost or market value. Accountants determine cost by using one of many methods, each based on a different assumption of cost flows. Typical cost flow assumptions include the following:

1.  Specific identification method—The actual cost of a particular inventory item is assigned to the item.

2.  Average cost method—Each item carries an equal cost, which is determined by dividing the total of the goods available for sale by the number of units to arrive at an average unit cost.

3.  First-in, first-out (FIFO)—The costs of the first items purchased are assigned to the first items sold and the costs of the last items purchased are assigned to the items remaining in inventory.

4.  Last-in, first-out (LIFO)—The costs of the last items purchased are assigned to the first items sold; the cost of the inventory on hand consists of the cost of items from the oldest purchases.

Major impacts of FIFO and LIFO inventory costing methods on financial statements in time of rising prices are shown here:

|                    | FIFO   | LIFO   |
| ------------------ | ------ | ------ |
| Ending inventory   | Higher | Lower  |
| Current assets     | Higher | Lower  |
| Working capital    | Higher | Lower  |
| Total assets       | Higher | Lower  |
| Cost of goods sold | Lower  | Higher |
| Gross margin       | Higher | Lower  |
| Net income         | Higher | Lower  |
| Taxable income     | Higher | Lower  |
| Income taxes       | Higher | Lower  |

The major accounting objective in selecting an inventory method should be to choose the one which, under the conditions and circumstances in practice, most clearly reflects periodic income.

An **accrued asset** or **accrued revenue** is a revenue for which the service has been performed or the goods have been delivered but that has not been recorded in the accounts, i.e., unrecorded revenue. For example, interest on a loan receivable is earned daily but may not actually be received until the following accounting period. On the balance sheet before the interest is received, unearned revenue would be reported as an asset. An adjusting entry would record the asset and the revenue.

**Prepaid expenses** are expenses of a future period that have been paid for but for which the company has not yet received benefits such as prepaid rent, prepaid insurance, or prepaid advertising. The benefits usually will be received in the next year. Prepaid expenses are assets, not expenses as the title might suggest.

**FINANCIAL ASSETS.** A financial asset entitles the owner to future cash flows to be paid by the issuer as well as to the liquidation value of the asset. The claim can be either an equity or debt claim. The price of any financial asset is equal to the present value of the cash flows expected. A derivative instrument is a contract whose value is related to the value of the underlying financial assets. Financial assets include financial instruments and securities. The entity that has agreed to make future cash payments is called the issuer of the financial assets; the owner of the financial asset is the investor.

Financial assets have characteristics that make them more or less attractive to investors and creditors: money equivalents, divisibility and denomination (size and dollar value), yield and return, term to maturity, liquidity, and risk. Risk is related to the variability of the price and the frequency of transactions at which buying and selling orders reach the market maker.

The basic economic functions of financial assets are to transfer funds from savers to investors and to redistribute the risk associated with the cash flow generated by the assets among parties seeking and those providing the funds. The major economic function of derivative instruments is to provide a method for controlling risk.

Financial instruments are complex and diversified. They also represent significant assets for many companies, especially for commercial banks, thrifts, brokerage firms, and insurance companies. Financial instruments includes trade receivables and payables, debt securities and common stock, many insurance contracts, financial futures and forward contracts, interest rate swaps and caps, collateralized mortgage obligations, and financial guarantees. Financial instruments may also include contracts that may not be recognized in financial statements at present—off-balance-sheet—such as financial guarantees, letters of credit, loan commitments, and obligations under operating leases.

Financial instruments have raised difficult accounting and reporting problems, including the following: off-balance-sheet financing, unjustifiable deferral of losses, premature recognition of gains, and inadequate disclosure about risks. Off-balance-sheet (OBS) risk exposes a company to a risk of accounting loss that exceeds the amount recognized for the instrument in the balance sheet.

*SFAS No. 105,* "Disclosure of Information about Financial Instruments with Off-Balance Sheet Risk and Financial Instruments with Concentration of Credit Risk," deals with reporting financial instruments in the balance sheet. Financial analysts should be familiar with this document. SFAS No. 105 requires that financial statements should provide significant information relating to all financial instruments with or without off-balance-sheet risk. The disclosures required by SFAS No. 105 should help financial statement users assess a company's risk of accounting loss associated with financial instruments: credit risk, market risk, risk of theft or physical loss, and the risk from a concentration of credit risk.

*SFAS No. 107,* "Disclosure about Fair Value of Financial Instruments," requires disclosure about fair value of all financial instruments, both assets and liabilities recognized and not recognized in the statement of financial positions of all firms.

The **fair value** of a financial instrument is the amount at which the instrument could be exchanged in a current transaction between willing parties, other than in forced or liquidation sale.

Certain factors may give rise to a difference between **book value** and **market value:** time to maturity; contractually fixed interest rates (coupon, loan, deposit, or borrowing rates); call provisions in bond indentures; possible loan prepayments; interest rate caps and floors; interest rate changes; and off-balance-sheet treatment.

**LONG-TERM INVESTMENTS.** Long-term investments in stocks, bonds, and other investments owned by a company that are to be held for a period of time exceeding the normal operating cycle of the business or one year, whichever is longer, are classified as investments on the balance sheet. Investments in common stock in which an investor is able to exercise significant influence over the operating and financial policies of an investee require the use of the equity method of accounting. An investment of 20 percent or more in the outstanding common stock of the investee is a presumption of significant influence. When the **equity method** is used, income from the investment is recorded by the investor when it is reported by the investee. The amount of the income recognized is based on the investor's percentage of ownership in the investee. Dividends are recorded as reductions in the carrying value of the investment account when they are paid by the investee.

To illustrate the equity method of accounting for an investment in common stock, assume that you purchased 20 percent of the outstanding stock of the ABC Company for $75,000. The ABC Company reported income of $100,000 for the year and paid a $10,000 cash dividend. The investor makes the following entries (1) to record the purchase of the stock, (2) to record income from the investment, and (3) to record the receipt of the cash dividend:

| | | |
|---|---|---|
| 1. Investment in Stock of ABC Company | 75,000 | |
|    Cash | | 75,000 |
| 2. Investment in Stock of ABC Company | 20,000 | |
|    Investment Income | | 20,000 |
| 3. Cash | 20,000 | |
|    Investment of Stock of ABC Company | | 2,000 |

The Investment in Stock of ABC Company would be reported on the balance sheet in the amount of $93,000 ($75,000 + $20,000 - $2,000). Investment income of $20,000 earned by the investee would be reported on the income statement of the investor.

**PROPERTY, PLANT, AND EQUIPMENT.** Property, plant, and equipment represent tangible, long-lived assets such as land, buildings, machinery, and tools acquired for use in normal business operations (and not primarily for sale) during a period of time greater than the normal operating cycle or one year, whichever is longer. **Accumulated depreciation** is a contra-asset account that represents the accumulation of charges resulting from allocating the cost of an asset over its useful life. The cost of the asset is decreased each year to reflect the effect of use, wear and tear, and obsolescence. The **book value** of the asset is the excess of its cost over its accumulated depreciation. The book value of an asset does not necessarily represent its fair market value or appraisal value.

    **Natural resources** or **wasting assets** represent inventories of raw materials that can be consumed (exhausted) through extraction or removal from their natural location. Natural resources include ore deposits, mineral deposits, oil reserves, gas deposits, and timber tracts. Natural resources are classified as a separate category within the property, plant, and equipment section. Natural resources are typically recorded at their acquisition cost plus exploration and development cost. Natural resources are subject to depletion. **Depletion** is the exhaustion of a natural resource that results from the physical removal of a part of the resource. On the balance sheet, natural resources are reported at total cost less accumulated depletion.

**INTANGIBLE ASSETS.** Intangible assets are long-lived assets representing nonphysical rights, values, privileges, and so on—exclusive of receivables and investments. Intangible assets include patents, copyrights, franchises, trademarks, trade names, goodwill, formulas, and other assets. **Goodwill** is the excess of the cost of an acquired business over the value assigned to the tangible and other identifiable intangible assets of the firm. Goodwill is recorded and reported only when it is acquired in the purchase of a business. **Research and development costs** (R&D) are those costs related to developing new products or processes, services, or techniques, or modifying existing ones. All research and development costs should be charged to expense when incurred. This practice suggests that the future expected value of R&D costs does not merit recognition as an asset because of the risks, uncertainties, and estimates involved. The cost of materials, equipment, and facilities that are acquired or constructed for R&D activities and that have alternative future uses should be capitalized when acquired or constructed. When such equipment and facilities are used, the depreciation of the items and materials consumed should be included as research and development costs.

**OTHER ASSETS.**   Assets that cannot be classified elsewhere on the balance sheet, including prepayments for services or benefits that affect the company over a future period greater than the period of time encompassed by the current asset classification, are reported as **other assets** or deferred charges. **Deferred charges** are long-term prepayments of expenses and include certain prepaid income taxes, bond issue costs, and benefits in the form of reduced future cash outflows for services. Deferred charges are similar to prepaid expenses. However, the benefit from such expenditures will be obtained over several years in the future.

**WORKING CAPITAL.**   Working capital is the excess of current assets over current liabilities. Adequate working capital is necessary for the business if it is to pay its debts as they come due. Creditors often consider working capital to constitute a margin of safety for paying short-term debts. Working capital assets are in a constant cycle of being converted into cash. Cash is used to acquire inventories that, when sold, become accounts receivable; receivables upon collection become cash; cash is used to pay current liabilities and expenses and to acquire more inventories. Working capital does not appear as a specific item on the balance sheet, but it can be computed as the difference between the reported current assets and current liabilities.

## LIABILITIES

**Liabilities** are probable future sacrifices of economic benefits arising from present obligations of a particular entity to transfer assets or provide services to other entities in the future as a result of past transactions or events.

Three essential characteristics of an accounting liability include the following:

1.  A duty or obligation to pay exists.
2.  The duty is virtually unavoidable by the entity.
3.  The event obligating the enterprise has occurred.

**CURRENT LIABILITIES.** Liabilities are usually classified as current or noncurrent liabilities. **Current liabilities** are those obligations whose liquidation is reasonably expected to require the use of existing resources, property classified as current assets, or the creation of other current liabilities. This definition emphasizes a short-term creditors' claim to working capital rather than the due date for classification purposes. Current liabilities include (1) trade accounts payable, (2) short-term notes payable, (3) current maturities of long-term liabilities, (4) unearned revenues (collections in advance, e.g., rent, interest, and magazine subscription revenues), (5) accrued expenses for payrolls, interest, taxes, and other expenses. **Unearned revenues** arise when assets are received before being earned; a liability called unearned revenue is created. After the services are performed, revenue is earned and the liability is settled. **Accrued liabilities** are liabilities that exist at the end of an accounting period but that have not yet been recorded. All liabilities not classified as current are reported as long-term liabilities.

**CONTINGENT LIABILITIES.** Contingent liabilities arise from an existing situation or set of circumstances involving uncertainty as to possible loss to an enterprise that will ultimately be resolved when one or more future events occur or fail to occur. Examples of contingent liabilities include product warranties and pending litigation. An estimated loss from a loss contingency must be accrued in the accounts and reported in financial statements as a charge against income and as a liability if both of the following conditions are met:

1.  It is probable that an asset has been impaired or a liability has been incurred at the date of the financial statements.
2.  The amount of the loss can be reasonably estimated.

If no loss accrual is required because one or both of the preceding conditions is not met but there is at least a *reasonable possibility* that a loss may have been incurred, the loss contingency should be disclosed in the notes to the financial statements. If the loss contingency is *remote*, disclosure is usually not required. Lawsuits represent contingencies that are often difficult to classify.

Obligations under mutually unexecuted contracts (executory contracts) such as those arising from purchase and employment commitments are usually not recognized as accounting liabilities.

**DEFERRED INCOME TAXES.** Federal, state, and local governments impose taxes against individuals, businesses, and other entities. Taxable income is determined by applying the tax rules and regulations. Because tax rules and regulations are used to compute taxable income and because accounting principles are used to compute income reported on financial statements, taxes payable can differ from the provision for income taxes (i.e., income-tax expense) reported on the income statement.

There are many temporary differences between transactions affecting income reported on the income statement and taxable income on the tax return. For example, a company purchases a plant asset in the current year and depreciates it in its financial statements using the straight-line method. On the tax return, the company depreciates the asset using the modified accelerated cost recovery method (MACRS). The first year's MACRS depreciation exceeds the straight-line amount. At the end of the current year, the book value of the related plant asset exceeds the asset's tax basis. The difference is only temporary because both the asset's book value and its tax basis will ultimately be zero (as the expensing of the asset is completed in the financial statements and on the tax return). In future year(s) when the temporary difference (excess of book value over tax basis) is expensed in the financial statements, the company will owe income taxes on the amount since there will not be a corresponding expense in that year's tax return. These deferred income taxes payable represent a *deferred tax liability*. Such differences can result in a special liability or deferred charge (asset) reported on the balance sheet. Accounting for these differences is generally accomplished by a process referred to as income-tax allocation (Source: *SFAS No. 109*, Accounting for Income Taxes).

To summarize, an accounting liability must be recognized when a temporary difference between an asset's book value and its tax basis will result in future taxable amounts. The deferred tax liability represents an estimate of future income taxes payable resulting from an existing temporary difference. The deferred tax liability is computed by applying the proper income-tax rates to the future taxable amounts.

The balance in a deferred tax liability or asset account on a balance sheet is the amount of taxes expected to be paid or refunded in the future as a result of the reversal (turnaround) of temporary differences existing at the balance sheet date.

A temporary difference originating in the current period that causes an increase in a deferred tax liability will cause a charge to the provision for deferred taxes (i.e., income-tax expense) on the income statement. An increase in a deferred tax asset will result in a reduction to the provision for deferred taxes.

When analyzing financial statements, the analysts should recognize that reporting for income taxes at the date of the financial statements includes the following balance sheet disclosures:

1.  A current tax liability or asset is recognized for the estimated taxes payable or refundable on the tax returns for the current year.

2.  A deferred tax liability or asset is recognized for the estimated future tax effects attributable to temporary differences and carryforwards.

3.  The measurement of current and deferred tax liabilities and assets is based on provisions of the enacted tax laws; the effects of future changes in tax laws or rates are not anticipated.

4.  The measurement of deferred tax assets is reduced, if necessary, by the amount of any tax benefits that, based on available evidence, are not expected to be realized.

A company must provide a reconciliation of the income-tax expense related to continuing operations with the income-tax expense that would result from applying federal tax rates to pretax income from continuing operations.

The following components of income-tax expense attributable to continuing operations must be disclosed, either in the financial statements or in disclosure notes:

1.  The current income-tax expense or benefit.

2.  The deferred tax expense or benefit.

3.  Any investment tax expense or benefit.

4.  Government grants to the extent they are used as reductions of income-tax expense.

5.  The benefits of operating loss carryforwards.

6.  Adjustments of deferred tax assets or liabilities as a result of enacted tax law or rate changes, or changes in the tax status of a firm.

If income-tax expense or benefit is allocated to items in addition to continuing operations (e.g., extraordinary items, discontinued operations, prior period adjustments), the amounts allocated separately to these additional items must be disclosed for each year for which those items are presented.

## *KEY DEFINITIONS*

*Deferred tax asset*—The amount of deferred tax consequences attributable to temporary differences that will result in net tax deductions in future years that could be recovered (based on operating loss carryback provisions in the tax law) by refund of taxes paid in the current or a prior year.

*Deferred tax liability*—The amount of deferred tax consequences attributable to temporary differences that will result in net taxable amounts in future years. The liability is the amount of taxes that would be payable on those net taxable amounts in future years based on the provisions of the currently enacted tax law.

*Income-tax expense (or benefit)*—The sum of income taxes payable (or refundable) and deferred tax expense (or benefit).

*Income taxes payable (or refundable)*—The amounts of income tax paid or payable (or refundable) for a year as determined by applying the provisions of the tax law to the taxable income or operating loss for that year. Sometimes called *current tax expense (or benefit)*.

*Liability/asset method*—Under the tax liability method of income-tax allocation (required according to generally accepted accounting principles), the deferred tax amount reported on the balance sheet is the effect of temporary differences that will reverse in the future and that are measured using the currently enacted income-tax rates and laws that will be in existence when the temporary differences reverse. The liability/asset method is balance-sheet-focused. Under the liability/liability method, the deferred tax consequences of temporary differences are recognizable liabilities and assets.

*Operating loss carryforward*—For financial reporting purposes, the amount of an operating loss carryforward for tax purposes (a) reduced by the amount that offsets temporary differences that will result in net taxable amounts during the carryforward period and (b) increased by the amount of temporary differences that will result in net tax deductions for which a tax benefit has not been recognized in the financial statements.

*Taxable income*—The excess of taxable revenues over tax-deductible expenses and exemptions for the year as defined by the governmental taxing authority.

*Temporary differences*—A difference between the tax basis of an asset or liability and its reported amount in the financial statements that will result in taxable or deductible amounts in future years when the reported amount of the asset or liability is recovered or settled, respectively. A temporary difference will result in either a tax liability that will be paid in the future or a prepaid tax that will result in a decrease in future tax payments at the then-current tax rate.

**PENSIONS.** A pension plan is an agreement between a company and its employee group whereby the company promises to provide income to its retired employees in return for the services that were provided by the employees during their employment. A *defined benefit plan* either specifically states the benefits to be received by employees after retirement or the method of determining such benefits. A *defined contribution plan* is one in which the employer's contribution is determined based on a specified formula, and any future benefits are limited to those that can be provided by the contributions and the returns earned on the investment of those contributions.

Pension plans may be either funded or unfunded. Under a funded plan, the company typically makes periodic payments to a funding agency that assumes the responsibility for safeguarding and investing the pension assets and for making payments to the recipients of benefits. An unfunded plan is one in which no periodic payments are made to an external agency; the pension payments to retired employees are made from current company resources. The amounts needed to fund a pension plan are determined by actuaries.

Pension cost (expense) reported on the income statement consists of several components, which include:

1. **Service cost.** The primary component of pension cost is the deferred compensation to be paid to employees in the future in return for their current services. The service cost is the actuarial present value of the benefits attributed by the pension benefit formula to services rendered by the employees during the current period.

2. **Interest expense.** Because employees' compensation is deferred until retirement, they are in effect providing a "loan" to the employer. The interest cost is the increase in the projected benefit obligation due to the passage of time. The interest on that loan is considered a component of pension cost. Projected benefit obligation is measured using assumptions concerning future compensation levels.

3. **Return on assets.** An employer generally invests its pension contributions into a pension fund with the intent that it earn a return on these assets. A negative component of pension cost is the return earned on the pension fund assets.

4. **Prior service cost.** When an employer begins a pension plan or makes modifications in its existing plan, additional benefits generally are due to employees as a result of their service performed in previous years. Part or all of the cost of these previously earned benefits can be a component of pension cost.

5.    **Gains and losses.** Unforeseen events related to a pension plan can result in a deviation in the current period between actual experience and the assumptions used and by changes in the assumptions about the future. Any resulting gains and losses can be a component of pension cost.

Pension plan liabilities are a form of deferred compensation. An unfunded accrued pension cost (a liability) is recognized and reported on the company's balance sheet if the net periodic pension expense recognized to date is greater than the amount funded to date. Alternatively, a prepaid pension cost (an asset) is recognized and reported on the company's balance sheet if the net periodic pension expense to date is less than the amount funded to date.

An additional liability may also have to be recognized if the accumulated benefit obligation is greater than the fair value of the plan assets at the end of the period. The accumulated benefit obligation is measured by using the actuarial present value of the benefits attributed by the pension benefit formula to employee services rendered before a specified date and based on employee services and compensation prior to that date. No assumption about future compensation levels is made. The unfunded accumulated benefit obligation is the minimum pension liability that the company must recognize. If this additional liability is recognized, a deferred pension cost (an intangible asset) of an equal amount is also recognized and reported on the company's balance sheet. The amount of the intangible asset must not exceed the amount of any unrecognized (unamortized) prior service cost. If the additional liability exceeds the unrecognized prior service cost, the excess is reported as a reduction of stockholders' equity.

To summarize, the pension liabilities, assets, and stockholders' equity items that can be reported on a company's balance sheet, depending on the circumstances, include:

| *Assets* | *Liabilities* |
|---|---|
| 1. Prepaid pension cost | 1. Unfunded accrued pension cost |
| 2. Intangible asset | 2. Additional pension liability |

*Stockholder's Equity*
1. Excess of additional pension liability over unrecognized prior
    service cost (a deduction)

A company with a defined benefit pension plan should make these additional disclosures:

1. A description of the plan including employee groups covered, type of benefit formula, funding policy, and types of assets held.

2. The amount of the pension expense showing separately the service cost components, the interest cost component, the actual return on assets for the period, and the net total of other components.

3. A schedule reconciling the funded status of the plan with amounts reported in the company's balance sheet, showing separately:

   a. The fair value of plan assets.

   b. The projected benefit obligation identifying the accumulated benefit obligation and the vested benefit obligation.

   c. The amount of unrecognized prior service cost.

   d. The amount of unrecognized gain or loss.

   e. The amount of any remaining unrecognized net obligation or net asset existing at the transition from *APB Opinion No. 8* to *FASB Statement No. 87.*

   f. The amount of any additional liability recognized.

   g. The amount of net pension asset or liability recognized in the balance sheet (the net of the previous six items).

4. The weighted average discount rate and rate of compensation increase used to measure the projected benefit obligation and the weighted average expected long-term rate of return on plan assets.

5. The amounts and types of securities included in plan assets.

## POST-RETIREMENT BENEFITS OTHER THAN PENSIONS.

Post-retirement benefits other than pensions include healthcare benefits, life insurance, legal assistance, tuition assistance, housing subsidies, day-care, and others. Such costs can result in major expenses being reported on the income statement. The basic accounting for such costs is similar to the principles used for pensions involving the concept of a liability existing before retirement. The post-retirement benefit expense reported on the income statement includes the following components, which are similar to those described for pension expense: service cost, interest cost, actual return on plan assets, amortization of unrecognized prior service cost, and gain or loss. A liability or asset would exist and be reported if the amount of the net post retirement benefit expense to date differs from the amount funded to date. No provision is required for recognizing an additional liability and the related intangible asset, as is required for pensions.

The financial statement disclosures required are similar to those for pensions along with additional information about the health cost trend rate used and sensitivity information about the effect of rate changes.

**LEASES.** The major reporting problem for **leases** is whether the lease should be included in the financial statements. A lease that transfers substantially all of the benefits and risks associated with ownership of the property should be accounted for as the acquisition of an asset and the incurring of an obligation by the lessee and as a sale or financing by the lessor. The criteria used to classify a lease as a **capital lease** for a lessee are the following four:

1. The lessor transfers ownership of the property to the lessee by the end of the lease term.

2. The lease contains a bargain purchase option.

3. The lease term is equal to 75 percent of the estimated economic life of the leased property.

4. The present value at the beginning of the lease term of the minimum lease payments excluding that portion representing executory costs equals or exceeds 90 percent of the fair market value of the property.

If a lease meets any one of the above criteria, it should usually be accounted for as a purchase by the lessee and a sale by the lessor. Otherwise it is considered an operating lease. Accounting for an operating lease merely involves the recognition of rent expense over the term of the lease by the lessee, as in the typical rental transaction. The lessor continues to carry on its balance sheet the leased assets, which it depreciates, and reports rent revenue when it is earned.

From the lessor's viewpoint, a nonoperating lease is either a **sales-type lease** or a **direct financing lease.** Sales-type leases involve a profit or loss to the lessor on the transfer of the asset to the lessee. Direct financing leases do not give rise to a profit or loss. Direct financing leases are essentially financing arrangements. Nonoperating leases must meet the four conditions for a capital lease by a lessee and two additional conditions:

1. Collectability of the minimum lease payment is reasonably predictable.

2. No important uncertainties surround the amount of unreimbursable costs yet to be incurred by the lessor.

A typical entry establishing a *lessee's* lease obligation for a **capital lease** is shown here:

| | | |
|---|---|---|
| Leased Equipment—Capital Lease (an asset) | 100,000 | |
|     Obligation under Capital Lease (a long-term liability) | | 100,000 |

The entry to record the periodic payment under the lease in which each payment represents a partial payment of the lease obligation and interest expense would be as follows:

| | | |
|---|---|---|
| Obligation under Capital Lease | xxxx | |
| Interest Expense | xxxx | |
|     Cash | | xxxx |

In a **direct financing lease,** the *lessor* would record the lease at its inception as follows:

| | | |
|---|---|---|
| Lease Receivable | xxxx | |
|     Unearned Interest Revenue | | xxxx |
|     Equipment | | xxxx |

Note that the lease receivable is recorded at the amount of the gross (undiscounted) rentals plus the estimated unguaranteed residual value of the leased asset. The equipment account is credited for the cost of the item to remove it from the lessor's books. Unearned interest revenue is the difference between the lease receivables and the carrying value of the equipment. The collection of the lease rentals and the recognition of interest revenue would be accomplished as follows:

| | | |
|---|---|---|
| 1. Cash | xxxx | |
|     Lease Receivable | | xxxx |
| 2. Unearned Interest Revenue | xxxx | |
|     Interest Revenue—Leases | | xxxx |

**LONG-TERM DEBT.** Long-term debt securities can be classified as (1) long-term notes and mortgages and (2) bonds payable. **Long-term notes** usually report the stated interest rate on an annual basis even though cash interest payments are made at more frequent intervals. Notes may be secured or unsecured. A **bond** is a legal instrument that represents a formal promise to pay (1) periodic interest on the principal and (2) a specified principal amount at a specified date in the future. Bonds have different characteristics depending on (1) the character of the issuing corporation, (2) security, (3) purpose of issue, (4) payment of interest, and (5) maturity of principal (term, serial, callable, redeemable, convertible). Premiums and discounts on bonds represent adjustments of the effective interest rate. The premium (discount) is amortized over the life of the issue, reducing (increasing) the coupon rate of interest to the effective interest rate incurred. The analyst is primarily interested in evaluating the terms of indebtedness, uncertainties related to the issue, and the coverage of interest charges. On a balance sheet, bond premiums and discounts are reported as adjustments of the face value of the bonds issued.

**MINORITY INTEREST.** Minority interest represents that portion of the stockholders' equity of a subsidiary not held by a parent or other member of the consolidated group. Minority interest is frequently reported on a consolidated balance sheet as a liability. However, minority interest does not meet the definition of a liability since a duty or obligation to pay does not exist. Some companies report minority interest in the stockholders' equity section of a consolidated balance sheet or in a section between liabilities and stockholders' equity.

## *STOCKHOLDERS' EQUITY*

**Equity** is the residual interest in the assets of an entity that remains after deducting its liabilities. In a business enterprise, the equity or capital is the ownership interest. In accounting for stockholders' equity, the basic accounting purposes are the following:

1. To identify the source of corporate capital.
2. To identify legal capital.
3. To indicate the dividends that could be distributed to the stockholders.

**PAID-IN OR CONTRIBUTED CAPITAL.** A distinction is usually made between capital originating from stockholders' investments, referred to as **contributed capital** or **paid-in capital,** and the equity originating from earnings, referred to as **retained earnings.** The stockholders' equity section of a corporate balance sheet is usually divided into three parts:

1. Capital stock—The par or stated value of the shares issued.
2. Additional paid-in capital—Primarily the excess of the amounts paid in over the par or stated value.
3. Retained earnings—The undistributed earnings of the corporation.

**Corporate capital stock** may be either preferred stock or common stock. **Preferred stock** usually has preferences over common stock relating to dividends and claims to assets if the corporation is dissolved. **Common stock** carries the right to vote in corporate affairs and to share in residual profits. A corporation may issue par value, stated value, or no-par capital stock. **Par value** or **stated value** refers to a specific dollar amount per share, which is printed on the stock certificate. Such values are frequently merely nominal amounts. The par or stated value of stock has no direct relationship to the share's market value. However, it frequently represents the corporation's **legal capital** as defined by state laws. **Legal capital** refers to the minimum amount that the corporation must hold and not pay out in dividends. **Additional paid-in capital** includes the excess of the price paid for the stock over its par or stated value.

**RETAINED EARNINGS.** Retained earnings represent the accumulated earnings of the corporation less dividends distributed to shareholders. A negative balance in the retained earnings account is referred to as a **deficit**. The retained earnings account does not represent cash or any other asset. The directors of a corporation may restrict, reserve, or *appropriate* retained earnings to show that these funds cannot be used to distribute assets as dividends. Retained earnings may be appropriated as a result of a legal, contractual, or discretionary requirement. The appropriation of retained earnings does not set aside or reserve cash or any other asset. The term **reserve** is used only to describe an appropriation of retained earnings. A reserve account for unspecified contingencies would be created by transferring an amount from retained earnings to the reserve account:

| | | |
|---|---|---|
| Retained Earnings | 50,000 | |
| Reserve (or Appropriation) for Contingencies | | 50,000 |

When the reason for which the appropriation was made no longer exists, the entry would simply be reversed to return the reserve to retained earnings.

**TREASURY STOCK.** Treasury stock represents a corporation's own stock that has been reacquired after having been issued and fully paid. Such reacquired shares are held in the treasury for reissue and are not retired. Treasury stock is not an asset. A corporation cannot recognize a gain or a loss when reacquiring or reissuing its own stock. Treasury stock does not possess voting rights, nor does it share in dividend distributions or in assets at liquidation of the enterprise. It is reported as a reduction of stockholders' equity in the stockholders' equity section of a balance sheet. Most state laws require that retained earnings be restricted in the amount of the cost of the treasury stock.

**STOCKHOLDERS' EQUITY ADJUSTMENTS.** When the financial statements of a foreign subsidiary are translated into dollars, **translation adjustments** resulting from restating the local currency–denominated balance sheets of foreign subsidiaries into dollars may arise, which must be disclosed and accumulated as a separate component of stockholders' equity. A strengthening of a foreign currency against the dollar enhances the U.S. dollar equivalent; a weakening has the opposite effect. The translation adjustment reflects the economic impact of exchange rate changes. The reported adjustment is an unrealized enhancement or reduction of stockholders' equity.

When the lower of cost or market method is used for noncurrent marketable equity securities, accumulated changes in the valuation allowance for such securities resulting from writing down or up (but not in excess of original cost) are included in the shareholders' equity section of the balance sheet and are shown separately. Such losses and recoveries are unrealized losses and recoveries.

## OFF-BALANCE-SHEET ITEMS

**Off-balance-sheet items** are sometimes encountered in financial statement analysis. Off-balance-sheet items generally refer to the application of procedures that provide financing without adding debt on a balance sheet, thus not affecting financial ratios or borrowing capacity of an enterprise. Off-balance-sheet items are often related to the sale of receivables with recourse, leases, take-or-pay contracts, and throughput arrangements.

Off-balance-sheet financing is often encountered when leasing transactions are structured as operating leases rather than capital leases when management's intent is to acquire an asset and incur a liability without recording either. Off-balance-sheet financing in such a situation would affect the computation of the debt/equity ratio. By avoiding the recording and reporting of a long-term liability, the company could avoid causing the debt part of the ratio to increase, which is an adverse development if the debt/equity ratio is currently high.

Banks often issue financial instruments that include contracts that may not be recognized in financial statements, such as financial guarantees, letters of credit, and loan commitments. Off-balance-sheet risk exposes a company to a risk of accounting loss that exceeds the amount recognized for the instrument in the balance sheet. Generally accepted accounting principles now require that financial statements provide significant information relating to all financial instruments with or without off-balance-sheet risk, including the following:

1.  Credit risk—maximum credit risk, probable and reasonably possible credit losses, and individual, industry, or geographic concentration of credit.

2.  Market risk—including interest rate and foreign exchange risks.

3.  Liquidity risk—resulting from inability to convert an instrument into cash.

## BALANCE SHEET USEFULNESS AND LIMITATIONS

The balance sheet provides a basis for evaluating a company's liquidity, financial flexibility, operating capabilities, and the earning performance for the period. Liquidity describes the amount of time that is expected to elapse until an asset is realized or otherwise converted into cash or until a liability has to be paid. Financial flexibility is the ability of an enterprise to take effective actions to alter the amounts and timing of cash flows so it can respond to unexpected needs and opportunities. Operating capabilities refer to the economic resources that a company can employ in its ongoing activities. Earning performance is a measure of the efficiency and effectiveness of a company in achieving its goals.

The balance sheet has major limitations. First, the balance sheet does not reflect current value or fair market value because accountants apply the historical cost principle in valuing and reporting assets and liabilities. Second, the balance sheet omits many items that have financial value to the business. For example, the value of the company's human resources, including managerial skills, is often significant but is not reported. In addition, professional judgment and estimates are often used in the preparation of balance sheets and can possibly impair the usefulness of the statements.

## THE INCOME STATEMENT

The **income statement** presents the results of operations for a reporting period. Exhibit 3.2 presents an income statement for the Mythical Manufacturing Company.

REVENUE – EXPENSES = NET INCOME

## Exhibit 3.2

### Mythical Manufacturing Company
### Consolidated Income Statement
### For the Years Ended December 31, 19X2 and 19X1
### (thousands of dollars)

|  | 19X2 | 19X1 |
|---|---|---|
| Net sales | $1,530,000 | $1,450,000 |
| Less cost of sales | 1,070,000 | 1,034,000 |
| Gross margin | 460,000 | 416,000 |
| Less operating expenses |  |  |
| Selling, general, and administrative expenses | 245,000 | 226,000 |
| Depreciation and amortization | 56,000 | 50,000 |
| Income from operations | 159,000 | 140,000 |
| Other income (expense) |  |  |
| Interest expense | (34,000) | (34,000) |
| Dividends and interest income | 12,000 | 19,000 |
| Income before income taxes | 137,000 | 125,000 |
| Less federal income taxes | 41,500 | 44,000 |
| Net income | $95,000 | $81,000 |
| Earnings per share of common stock | $3.16 | $2.77 |

The income statement provides information concerning return on investment, risk, financial flexibility, and operating capabilities. Return on investment is a measure of a firm's overall performance. **Risk** is the uncertainty associated with the future of the enterprise. **Financial flexibility** is the firm's ability to adapt to problems and opportunities. **Operating capability** relates to the firm's ability to maintain a given level of operations.

**CONTENTS.** An income statement should reflect all items of profit and loss recognized during the period, except for a few items that would go directly to retained earnings, notably prior-period adjustment (mainly the correction of errors of prior periods). The following summary illustrates the income statement currently considered to represent generally accepted accounting principles:

Revenues
Deduct: Cost of goods sold and expenses
Income from continuing operations
Discontinued operations
Extraordinary gains and losses
Cumulative effect of change in accounting principle
Net income

Generally accepted accounting principles require disclosing **earnings-per-share** amounts on the income statement of all publicly reporting entities. Earnings-per-share data provide a measure of the enterprise's management and past performance and enable users of financial statements to evaluate future prospects of the enterprise and assess dividend distributions to shareholders. Disclosure of earnings-per-share effects of discontinued operations and extraordinary items is optional but is required for income from continuing operations, income before extraordinary items, cumulative effect of a change in accounting principle, and net income. In certain cases, earnings-per-share data must be presented for (1) primary earnings per share and (2) fully diluted earnings per share. **Primary earnings per share** is a presentation based on the outstanding common shares and those securities that are in substance equivalent to common shares and have a diluting effect. Convertible bonds, convertible preferred stock, stock options, and warrants are examples of common stock equivalents. The **fully diluted earnings-per-share** presentation is a pro forma presentation that affects the dilution of earnings per share that would have occurred if all contingent issuances of common stock that would individually reduce earnings per share had taken place at the beginning of the period.

**REVENUES AND EXPENSES.** On an income statement, **sales** refers to the total amount charged to customers as the sales prices of products sold during the accounting period. Sales discounts and sales returns and allowances are usually shown as adjustments to total sales.

**Cost of goods sold** refers to the cost to the business of the merchandise sold to customers during the period. The accounting method adopted for inventory can have a significant impact on cost of goods sold. Cost of goods sold is computed as follows:

| | |
|---|---:|
| Inventory at the beginning of the period | $100,000 |
| Purchases (net of discounts, returns, allowances) | 785,000 |
| Goods available for sale | 885,000 |
| Deduct: Inventory at the end of the period | 75,000 |
| Cost of goods sold | $810,000 |

Operating expenses include those costs incurred in normal profit-directed operations, such as selling expenses and general and administrative expenses. **Depreciation** is an operating expense. Depreciation is the result of the accounting process of allocating the cost or other basic value of a tangible, long-lived asset or group of assets less salvage value, if any, over the estimated useful life of the asset(s) in a systematic and rational manner. Recording depreciation does not establish the market value of the related asset. Depreciation charges are noncash expenses that reduce net income. The depreciation allowance is not a cash fund accumulated to cover the replacement cost of an asset. Two major depreciation methods are frequently used by companies to compute depreciation expense:

1. **Straight-line depreciation,** which allocates the cost of the asset, less any salvage value, equally over the life of the asset.

2. **Accelerated depreciation,** which charges a greater proportion of the asset's total depreciation during the early years of its life than during the later years.

The analyst needs to know the reasonableness of the company's depreciation policy as well as the depreciation method used and their impact on net income and income taxes.

**Other revenue and expenses** include items arising from transactions not directly related to normal operations. Other revenue and expenses include dividends and interest received from stocks or bonds owned, income from rents and royalties, gains and losses on sale of assets, and other items.

**DISCONTINUED OPERATIONS.** Discontinued operations are those operations of an enterprise that have been sold, abandoned, or otherwise disposed of. The results of continued operations must be reported separately in the income statement from discontinued operations, and any gain or loss from the disposal of a segment must be reported along with the operating results of the discontinued segment. A segment of a business is a component of an entity whose activities represent a separate major line of business or class of customer.

**EXTRAORDINARY ITEMS.** Extraordinary items are material events and transactions that are both unusual in nature and infrequent in occurrence. Extraordinary items could result if gains or losses were the direct result of any of the following events or circumstances:

1. A major casualty, such as an earthquake.

2. An expropriation of property by a foreign government.

3. A prohibition under a newly enacted law or regulation.

Extraordinary items are shown net of applicable income taxes.

**ACCOUNTING CHANGES.** An **accounting change** refers to a change in accounting principle, accounting estimate, or reporting entity. **Changes in accounting principle** result when an accounting principle is adopted that is different from the one previously used. For example, a change in depreciation from the straight-line method to the double-declining method would be considered a change in accounting principle. The net effect on net income of adopting the new accounting principle must be disclosed as a separate item following extraordinary items on the income statement. A change from one accounting principle to another is justified if management believes that the adopted principle is to be preferred. **Changes in estimate** involve revision of estimates, such as useful lives or residual value of depreciable assets, the loss for bad debts, and warranty costs. In such cases, prior period statements are not adjusted; the new estimate is used over the current and future periods. A **change in reporting entity** occurs when a company changes its composition from the prior period, as occurs when a new subsidiary is acquired. Changes in a reporting entity require that financial statements of all prior periods presented be restated to show financial information for the new reporting entity for all periods.

**IMPLICATIONS FOR ANALYSTS.** When analyzing the income statements, the analyst is primarily interested in (1) identifying the components of income change, (2) determining the profitability trend, and (3) estimating the sensitivity of income to operating and economic factors.

The income statement has some limitations. Among other things, the income statement does not include many items that contribute to the earnings of an enterprise, especially items that cannot be quantified. In addition, the income numbers reported on income statements are often the result of accounting methods employed by the accountant in preparing the statements. Accounting methods can affect the quality of earnings reflected on the income statement.

## *STATEMENT OF CASH FLOWS*

The statement of cash flows is a report providing information about a company's cash receipts and payments during a period. The statement is useful in assessing a company's ability to generate future net cash inflows, appraising the company's ability to pay debts and dividends, evaluating the company's requirements for external financing, reconciling the differences between net income reported on the income statement and related cash flows from operating activities, and evaluating the cash and noncash impact of the company's investing and financing activities during the period.

The statement of cash flows explains the change in a company's cash during a period. If a company invests in highly liquid short-term investments, the statement explains the changes during the period in cash and cash equivalents.

The statement of cash flows is classified into three categories: operating, investing, and financing activities. Operating activities include producing or delivering goods for sale and providing services. Cash flows from operating activities generally include the cash receipts and disbursements from transactions and other events that enter into the determination of net income. Investing activities include (1) acquiring and selling plant assets and securities that are not considered to be cash equivalents and (2) lending money and collecting on the principal amounts of these loans. Financing activities include (1) obtaining resources from owners and providing them with a return on their investment (dividend payments) and (2) obtaining resources from creditors and repaying the principal amounts borrowed.

Investing and financing activities that provide both cash receipts and cash payments during an accounting period are reported separately on the statement. For example, if a company issues long-term debt to retire maturing debt, the cash proceeds from new issuances of long-term debt should be reported separately from cash payments for maturing debt issues. Exhibit 3.3 indicates the relations of the four primary financial statements provided in an annual report to stockholders.

## Exhibit 3.3

### Relationship of Financial Statements

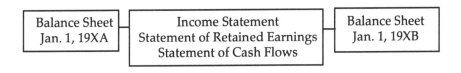

| Balance Sheet Jan. 1, 19XA | Income Statement Statement of Retained Earnings Statement of Cash Flows | Balance Sheet Jan. 1, 19XB |

Significant investing and financing activities of a company during a period affect assets or liabilities on the balance sheet but do not result in cash
flows in the period. These noncash investing and financing activities must
generally be disclosed in the form of a narrative discussion or a supplemen-
tal schedule to the statement of cash flows.

A simplified statement of cash flows is illustrated in Exhibit 3.4 along
with two supplementary schedules.

## Exhibit 3.4

**Cash-Flow Statement and Supplementary Schedules**
**Mythical Manufacturing Company**
**STATEMENT OF CASH FLOWS**
**For the Year Ended December 31, 19X5**
**(Amounts in thousands)**

| | |
|---|---:|
| *Cash flows from operating activities* | |
| Cash received from customers | $1,600 |
| Cash paid to suppliers | 500 |
| Cash paid to employees | 500 |
| Cash paid for taxes | 50 |
| Net cash provided by operating activities | 550 |
| | |
| *Cash flows from investing activities* | |
| Purchases of machinery | (900) |
| Proceeds from sale of land | 200 |
| Net cash used by investing activities | (700) |
| | |
| *Cash flows from financing activities* | |
| Proceeds of bond issuance | 350 |
| Payment to retire bonds | (200) |
| Proceeds from issuing common stock | 200 |
| Payment of dividends | (250) |
| Net cash provided by financing activities | 100 |
| Net decrease in cash | $(50) |
| | |
| Cash January 1, 19X5 | 200 |
| Cash December 31, 19X5 | $150 |

## Schedule 1
### Reconciliation of net income to net cash provided by operating activities

| | |
|---|---:|
| Net income | $500 |
| Adjustments to reconcile net income to cash provided by operating activities: | |
| Depreciation expense | (300) |
| Decrease in accounts receivable | (100) |
| Increase in accounts payable | (50) |
| Net cash provided by operating activities | $550 |

## Schedule 2
### Noncash investing and financing activities

| | |
|---|---:|
| Purchase of building through issuance of long-term note | $100,000 |
| Conversion of bonds into shares of common stock | $50,000 |

*A more detailed discussion of the cash flows statement is presented in Chapter 8.*

# RETAINED EARNINGS STATEMENT

The **retained earnings statement** reconciles the beginning and ending balances in the retained earnings account. Exhibit 3.5 presents a retained earnings statement for the Mythical Manufacturing Company. This statement can be presented as a separate statement or in a combined statement of income and retained earnings. A retained earnings statement reporting a prior-period adjustment would appear as follows:

| | |
|---|---:|
| Beginning retained earnings | $100,000 |
| Deduct: Adjustment for failure to record depreciation in prior year | 10,000 |
| Adjusted beginning retained earnings | 90,000 |
| Add: Net income for the period | 200,000 |
| | 290,000 |
| Deduct: Dividends | 30,000 |
| Retained earnings at end of year | $260,000 |

## Exhibit 3.5

### Mythical Manufacturing Company
### Retained Earnings Statement
### December 31, 19X2 and 19X1
### (thousands of dollars)

|                              | 19X2      | 19X1      |
| ---------------------------- | --------- | --------- |
| Balance January 1            | $439,200  | $393,700  |
| Net income                   | 95,500    | 81,000    |
| Total                        | 534,700   | 474,700   |
| Less:                        |           |           |
| Dividends on preferred stock | 700       | 700       |
| Dividends on common stock    | 36,000    | 34,800    |
| Balance on December 31       | $498,000  | $439,200  |

A few profit-and-loss items are reported as **prior period adjustments** on financial statements and require a restatement of the opening balance of retained earnings. These items are primarily corrections of errors from a prior period. Material errors in the financial statement of one accounting period that are discovered in a subsequent period usually involve an asset or liability and a revenue or expense of a prior year. In the year of the correction, the asset or liability account balance should be corrected and the related revenue or expense should be made directly to the retained earnings account and should not affect the income statement for the period. If comparative financial statements are presented, the prior year statements should be restated to show the effect on net income, retained earnings, and asset or liability balances for all periods reported. In addition to prior-period adjustments, certain accounting changes that require statements of prior period financial statements are also reported on the statement of retained earnings.

A dividend is a distribution of cash, other assets, liabilities, or a company's own stock to stockholders in proportion to the number of shares owned. The distribution is usually generated from earnings of the corporation. The board of directors of a corporation is responsible for determining dividend policy including the amount, timing, and type of dividends to be declared. The types of dividends can be classified as follows:

1. Dividends that decrease total stockholders' equity:

    a. Cash dividends

b. Property dividends

c. Script dividends

2. Dividends not affecting total stockholders' equity:

a. Stock dividends

b. "Dividends" not affecting any stockholders' equity account (stock splits in the form of a dividend)

A stock dividend is the issuance by a corporation of its own shares of common stock to its common stockholders with consideration. Corporations sometimes issue stock dividends when they want to make a distribution to their stockholders but either do not want to distribute assets or do not have enough assets to distribute. Stock dividends have also been used to reduce the market value of a corporation's stock, thereby making it available to a larger number of potential investors and hopefully increasing the demand for the stock. The net assets of the corporation are not affected by the distribution of a stock dividend.

A **stock split** is a distribution of a company's own capital stock to existing stockholders with the purpose of reducing the market price of the stock, which hopefully increases the demand for the shares. After a stock split, the components of stockholders' equity are the same as before the split. Only the par value of the shares and the number of shares outstanding have changed.

## THE AUDITOR'S REPORT

An audit and the **auditor's report** provide additional assurance to users of financial statements concerning the information presented in the statement. The **attest function** of external auditing refers to the auditor's expressing an opinion on a company's financial statements. Generally, the criteria for judging an auditee's financial statements are generally accepted accounting principles. The typical audit leads to an attestation regarding the fairness and dependability of the financial statements, which is communicated to the officials of the audited entity in the form of a written report that accompanies the financial statements.

The auditor's report is typically the last item presented in the financial statements, although it can precede the financial reports. The auditor has sole responsibility for the opinion expressed in the auditor's report. Company management has the primary responsibility for the financial statements themselves, including supporting notes. Auditors give their opinion to affirm or disaffirm what management has compiled and presented. Six required elements in the auditor's report have special significance:

1.  Date

2.  Salutation (to whom addressed)

3.  Identification of the statements examined

4.  Statement regarding the scope of the examination

5.  Reference to fair presentation in conformity with generally accepted accounting principles

6.  Signature of the CPA

A typical *unqualified audit opinion* is one in which the auditor has no reservations concerning the financial statements. An audit report expressing an unqualified opinion contains three paragraphs. The first paragraph, known as the introductory paragraph, lists the financial statements that were audited, states that management is responsible for those statements, and asserts that the auditor is responsible for expressing an opinion on them.

The second paragraph, referred to as the scope paragraph, describes what the auditor has done. It states that the auditor has examined the financial statements in accordance with generally accepted auditing standards and has performed appropriate tests.

The third paragraph, known as the opinion paragraph, gives the auditor's opinion regarding the financial statements described in the introductory paragraph, i.e., that they are presented fairly in conformity with generally accepted accounting principles.

In other circumstances, a **modified opinion**, a **qualified opinion**, an **adverse opinion**, or a **disclaimer of opinion** might be expressed. A modified report includes a fourth explanatory paragraph. The two most common types of modified reports are the result of material uncertainties and changes in accounting principles. A qualified opinion states that except for the effects of the qualified item, the financial statements present fairly the information in conformity with GAAP. An adverse opinion states that the financial statements do not present fairly the information in conformity with GAAP. A disclaimer of opinion states that the auditor does not express an opinion.

The standard format of an unqualified auditor's report is shown in Exhibit 3.6.

The independent audit report sets forth the independent auditor's **unqualified opinion** regarding the financial statements if they are presented fairly in conformity with generally accepted accounting principles applied on a basis consistent with that of the preceding year. A fair presentation of

## Exhibit 3.6

## Independent Auditor's Report

To the Stockholders and Board of Directors of Merck & Co., Inc.:

We have audited the accompanying consolidated balance sheets of Merck & Co., Inc. (a New Jersey Corporation) and Subsidiaries as of December 31, 19X2 and 19X1, and the related statements of income, retained earnings, and cash flows for each of the three years in period ended December 31, 19X2. These financial statements are the responsibility of the Company's management. Our responsibility is to express an opinion on these financial statements based on our audits.

We conducted our audits in accordance with generally accepted auditing standards. Those standards require that we plan and perform the audit to obtain reasonable assurance about whether the financial statements are free of material misstatement. An audit includes examining, on a test basis, evidence supporting the amounts and disclosures in the financial statements. An audit also includes assessing the accounting principles used and significant estimates made by management, as well as evaluating the overall financial statement presentation. We believe that our audits provide a reasonable basis for our opinion.

In our opinion, the financial statements referred to above present fairly, in all material respects, the financial position of Merck & Co., Inc. and Subsidiaries as of December 31, 19X2 and 19X1, and the results of its operations and its cash flows for each of the three years in the period ended December 31, 19X2, in conformity with generally accepted accounting principles.

New York, New York
January 23, 19X3

---

financial statements is generally understood by accountants to refer to whether:

1. The accounting principles used in the statements have general acceptability.

2. The accounting principles are appropriate in the circumstances.

The fair presentation of financial statements does not mean that the statements are fraud-proof. The independent auditor has the responsibility to search for errors or irregularities within the recognized limitations of the auditing process. An auditor understands that the audit was based on selective testing and was subject to risks that material errors or irregularities, if they exist, will not be detected.

## THE ANNUAL REPORT

A typical annual report includes the chief executive officer's letter to the stockholders along with statistical data on a three-year comparative basis, including such items as earnings per share, sales volume, dividends per share, return on investment, net income as a percentage of sales, and the current ratio. In addition, a 5- or 10-year summary of important statistical data is presented following the financial statements. These two statistical summaries are not covered by the auditor's opinion.

In a typical report, management includes an analysis of the current and previous years, which is referred to as the "Management's Discussion and Analysis." In this section, management discusses the company's operations, financial position, and other important matters. The analyst should read this section with caution.

## SUMMARY

The information presented in financial statements is primarily financial in nature, i.e., it is quantifiable and is expressed in units of money. The numbers are usually based on exchange prices. The information often reflects approximations rather than exact measurements. Information presented on financial statements typically reflects the effects of transactions, events, and circumstances that have already happened, i.e., historical data. Analysts should not rely completely on financial statements when making economic decisions about a business enterprise but should consider other factors such as general economic conditions, political events, and industry outlook.

# Chapter 4

# AN OVERVIEW OF FINANCIAL STATEMENT ANALYSIS

**Financial statement analysis** involves tools and techniques that enable analysts to examine past and current financial statements so that a company's performance and financial position can be evaluated and future risks and potential estimated. Financial statement analysis can yield valuable information about trends and relationships, the quality of a company's earnings, and the strengths and weaknesses of its financial position.

## BASIC CONSIDERATIONS

Financial statement analysis begins with establishing the objective(s) of the analysis. For example, is the analysis undertaken to provide a basis for granting credit or making an investment? After the objective of the analysis is established, the data are accumulated from the financial statements and from other sources. The results of the analysis are summarized and interpreted. Conclusions are reached and a report is made to the person(s) for whom the analysis was undertaken. To evaluate financial statements, a person must:

1.   Be acquainted with business practices.

2.   Understand the purpose, nature, and limitations of accounting.

3.   Be familiar with the terminology of business and accounting.

4.   Have a working knowledge of the fundamentals of finance.

5.   Be acquainted with the tools of financial statement analysis.

Financial analysis of a company should include an examination of the financial statements of the company, including notes to the financial statements, and the auditor's report. The auditor's report will state whether the financial statements have been audited. The report also indicates whether the statements fairly present the company's financial position, results of operations, and changes in financial position in accordance with generally accepted accounting principles on a basis consistent with the preceding year.

**Notes** to the financial statements are often more meaningful than the date found within the body of the statements. The notes explain the accounting policies of the company and usually provide detailed explanations of how those policies were applied along with supporting details.

Analysts often compare the financial statements of one company with those of other companies in the same industry and of the industry in which the company operates as well as with prior year statements of the company being analyzed. This procedure substantially broadens the scope of financial statement analysis.

## MAJOR TOOLS OF ANALYSIS

Accountants and others have developed a variety of standardized tools and techniques that can be used in financial statement analysis. Financial statement procedures fall into three basic categories: (1) comparisons and measurements relating to financial data for two or more periods, (2) comparisons and measurements relating to financial data of the current period, and (3) special-purpose examinations. A review of financial statements can involve all three types of analysis. The following analytical tools will be discussed in this chapter to provide an overview of financial statement analysis:

1.   Comparative financial statements:

     a.   Horizontal analysis

     b.   Vertical analysis

2.   Common-size financial statements

3.   Ratio analysis

4.   Special-purpose examinations

Additional tools of analysis will be presented in subsequent chapters.

## COMPARATIVE FINANCIAL STATEMENTS

Financial statements presenting financial data for two or more periods are called **comparative statements.** Comparative financial statements usually give similar reports for the current period and for one or more preceding periods. Comparative financial statements provide analysts with significant information about **trends** and **relationships** over two or more years. Comparative statements are considerably more significant than are single-year statements. Comparative statements emphasize the fact that financial statements for a single accounting period are only one part of the continuous history of the company.

Comparisons between financial statements are most informative and useful under the following conditions, according to the Accounting Principles Board:

1.   The presentations are in good form; that is, the arrangements within the statement are identical.

2.   The content of the statements is identical; that is, the same items from the underlying accounting records are classified under the same captions.

3.   Accounting principles are not changed or, if they are changed, the financial effects of the changes are disclosed.

4.   Changes in circumstances or in the nature of the underlying transactions are disclosed.

**HORIZONTAL ANALYSIS. Horizontal analysis** spotlights trends and establishes relationships between items that appear on the same row of a comparative statement. Horizontal analysis discloses changes on items in financial statements over time. Each item (such as sales) on a row for one fiscal period is compared with the same item in a different period. Horizontal analysis can be carried out in terms of changes in dollar amounts, in percentages of change, or in a ratio format.

Exhibit 4.1 illustrates horizontal analysis on a balance sheet. The **amount of change** is computed by subtracting the amount for the base year (19X2) from the amount for the current year (19X3). The **percentage of change** is computed by dividing the amount of change by the base year. The **year-to-year** ratio is computed by dividing the current year data by the base year data. When the base figure is a positive value, the dollar change and the percentage change can be computed validly. If the base figure is zero or a negative value, the dollar change can be computed but the percentage change cannot. A ratio can be computed only when two positive values are available. Where changes are expressed as percentages, no vertical addition

## Exhibit 4.1

### Horizontal Analysis of a Balance Sheet
### HORIZONTAL COMPANY
### Statement of Financial Position
### December 31, 19X3 to 19X2

|  | 19X3 | 19X2 | Amount of Change | Percentage of Change | Ratio 19X3 to 19X2 |
|---|---|---|---|---|---|
| **Assets** |  |  |  |  |  |
| Cash | $15,000 | $10,000 | $5,000 | 50.0% | 1.50 |
| Accounts receivable | 5,000 | 10,000 | (5,000) | (50.0) | 0.50 |
| Inventory | 30,000 | — | 30,000 | — | — |
| Property, plant, and equipment | 125,000 | 150,000 | (25,000) | (16.7) | 0.83 |
| Total assets | $175,000 | $170,000 | $5,000 | 2.9 | 1.03 |
| **Liabilities** |  |  |  |  |  |
| Accounts payable | $15,000 | — | $15,000 | — | — |
| Bonds payable | — | $100,000 | (100,000) | (100.0) | 0.00 |
| **Owner's Equity** |  |  |  |  |  |
| Common Stock | 155,000 | 80,000 | 75,000 | 93.8 | 1.94 |
| Retained earnings | 5,000 | (10,000) | 15,000 | — | — |
| Total liabilities and owner's equity | $175,000 | $170,000 | $5,000 | 2.9 | 1.03 |

or subtraction of the percentages can be made because the percentages of change are the results of different bases. When individual items have small base amounts, a relatively small dollar change can result in a significant percentage change, thereby assigning more importance to the item than might be meaningful.

A **base-year-to-date** approach to horizontal analysis is sometimes used to disclose the cumulative percentage changes. When this approach is used, the *initial* year is used as the base year, and the cumulative results from subsequent years are compared with the initial year to determine the cumulative percentage changes.

**VERTICAL ANALYSIS.** Vertical analysis involves the conversion of items appearing in statement **columns** into terms of percentages of a base figure to show the relative significance of the items and to facilitate comparisons. For example, individual items appearing on the income statement can be expressed as percentages of sales. On the balance sheet, individual assets can be expressed in terms of their relationship to total assets. Liabilities and shareholders' equity accounts can be expressed in terms of their relationship to total liabilities and shareholders' equity. On a statement of changes in financial position, the increase in cash (or working capital) is usually expressed as 100 percent. On the retained earnings statement, beginning retained earnings is 100 percent. Exhibit 4.2 illustrates vertical analysis of an income statement.

## COMMON-SIZE STATEMENTS

Statements omitting dollar amounts and showing only percentages are referred to as common-size statements because each item in the statement has a common basis for comparison, for example, total assets or net sales. Data for common-size statements are computed in a manner similar to that described for vertical analysis computations. Changes in proportions are emphasized in common-size statements, which make efficiencies and inefficiencies easier to identify than in comparative statements. For example, sales salaries will indicate the percentage of each sales dollar they took each year. Exhibit 4.3 illustrates a common-size statement.

When analyzing the balance sheet, common-size statements are useful in examining the sources and structure of capital of the enterprise, that is, the

**Exhibit 4.2**

**Vertical Analysis of an Income Statement**
**VERTICAL COMPANY**
**Income Statement**
**For the Year Ended December 31, 19X1**

|  |  | Percentage of Net Sales |
|---|---|---|
| Sales (net) | $200,000 | 100.0% |
| Cost of goods sold | 50,000 | 25.0 |
| Gross margin on sales | 150,000 | 75.0 |
| Operating expenses | 100,000 | 50.0 |
| Net operating income | 50,000 | 25.0 |
| Federal income tax | 25,000 | 12.5 |
| Net income | $25,000 | 12.5% |

---

**Exhibit 4.3**

---

**Common-Size Statement**

**Common-Size Company**
**Income Statement**
**For the Years Ended December 31, 19X2 and 19X1**

|                                                   | 19X2   | 19X1   |
|---------------------------------------------------|--------|--------|
| Sales                                             | 100.0% | 100.0% |
| Operating costs                                   |        |        |
| Cost of sales                                     | 80.9%  | 80.7%  |
| Selling, general, and administrative expenses     |        |        |
| Pensions                                          | 10.2   | 9.9    |
| State and local taxes                             | 1.9    | 2.0    |
| Total operating costs                             | 97.4%  | 99.2%  |
| Net income                                        | 2.6%   | 0.8%   |

---

relationship of liabilities and equity capital. Also, the analysis provides information concerning the distribution of assets among current assets, investments, property, plant, and equipment, intangible assets, and other assets. Common-size income statements provide information concerning what proportion of the sales dollar is absorbed by cost of goods sold and various expenses. On comparative, common-size statements, the comparisons demonstrate the changing or stable relationships within groups of assets, liabilities, revenues, expenses, and other financial statement categories. Care must be exercised when such comparisons are made since the percentage change can result from a change in the absolute amount of the item or a change in the total of the group of which it is a part, or both.

Common-size statements are useful in comparing companies because such statements are based on 100 percent and present a relative comparison instead of absolute amounts. Such intercompany comparisons can help the analysts identify variations in structure or distributions among groups and subgroups.

## RATIO ANALYSIS

A **ratio** is an expression of a mathematical relationship between one quantity and another. The ratio of 400 to 200 is 2:1 or 2. If a ratio is to have any utility, the elements that constitute the ratio must express a meaningful relationship. For example, there is a relationship between accounts receivable and sales, between net income and total assets, and between current assets and current liabilities. Ratio analysis can disclose relationships that reveal conditions and trends that often cannot be noted by inspection of the individual components of the ratio.

Ratios are generally not significant of themselves but assume significance when they are compared with (1) previous ratios of the same firm, (2) some predetermined standard, (3) ratios of other enterprises in the same industry, or (4) ratios of the industry within which the company operates. When used in this manner, ratios serve as "benchmarks" against which the company can evaluate itself. Ratios are not ends in themselves but help provide answers to questions concerning specific issues and insights into the operations of a business enterprise.

When using ratios, analysts must understand the factors that enter into the structure of the ratio and the way changes in such factors influence the ratio. For example, what impact does borrowing money from a bank have on the current ratio? Will it increase, decrease, or have no impact on the ratio? If the objective is to improve the ratio, what changes can be made in the components of the ratio to accomplish the desired goal?

**MATHEMATICAL CAUTIONS.** Care must be taken in projecting the effect on a ratio of a change in the numerator or denominator of a ratio. For example,

1. If a ratio is less than 1.00 (numerator is smaller than the denominator), equal increases in both quantities in the ratio would cause the ratio to increase. For example, $3/4 = 0.75$ and $(3 + 1)/(4 + 1) = 4/5 = 0.80$. Similarly, equal decreases in both numerator and denominator would cause the ratio to decrease.

2. If the value of a ratio is greater than 1.00, equal increases in both quantities in the ratio would cause the ratio to decrease. For example, $4/3 = 1.33$ and $(4 + 1)/(3 + 1) = 5/4 = 1.25$. Equal decreases in both numerator and denominator would cause the ratio to increase.

3. If the value of a ratio is exactly 1.00, equal changes in the numerator and denominator will have no effect on the ratio, which remains at 1.00.

4. If the numerator increases (decreases) with no change in the denominator, the ratio would increase (decrease).

5. If the denominator increases (decreases) with no change in the numerator, the ratio would decrease (increase).

6.   If the numerator and denominator change but in unequal amounts, the ratio will increase, decrease, or remain unchanged depending upon the direction and the amount of the change.

**IMPLICATIONS FOR ANALYSIS.** In ratio analysis, the analyst identifies deviations in computed ratios and then examines the causes of the deviations. For example, deviations from industry norms could indicate that the firm was doing something different from the average enterprise in the industry, excluding businesses that did not survive.

Ratios should be used with caution. In and of themselves, ratios generally should not be the sole basis for decision making. They should be treated as additional evidence (not conclusive evidence) leading to a decision or solution.

Ratios are only as relevant and reliable as the data that goes into them. One must constantly keep in mind that while financial statements are prepared according to generally accepted accounting principles, the statements reflect estimates and judgments that may or may not be particularly relevant in an analysis that is directed toward a particular objective.

At times ratios are difficult to interpret. For example, exactly what does a 2:1 ratio mean? Is it good or bad, favorable or unfavorable? Comparing ratios with some standard, such as those of preceding years, other companies, or the industry, can provide some guidance.

The analyst should understand that ratios have certain limitations in addition to those mentioned above, including the following:

1.   Ratios reflect past conditions, transactions, events, and circumstances.

2.   Ratios reflect book values, not real economic values or price-level effects.

3.   The computation of ratios is not completely standardized.

4.   The application of accounting principles and policies varies among firms, and changes in their application from period to period affect the ratios.

5.   Intercompany comparisons are difficult when companies are diversified or have different risk characteristics.

In spite of the difficulties associated with the formation and interpretation of ratios, ratio analysis is an important technique for financial statement analysis because it can identify significant fundamental and structural relationships and trends.

Computerized data bases that contain financial information on many companies is commercially available from several firms. For example, Compustat data base is marketed by Standard & Poor's. This data base contains information on over 120 items for over 2,500 industrial companies. Although such data bases have certain theoretical and practical problems related to their use, they can provide the analyst with valuable source material in many instances.

## *SPECIALIZED ANALYTICAL TOOLS*

In addition to comparative statements, common-size statements, and ratio analysis, analysts have many specialized tools and techniques they can apply to special-purpose studies. Such studies could include factors such as insurance coverage, the seasonal nature of the business, segment data, foreign operations, concentration of sales within a small number of customers, unusual events affecting the company, and the effect of inventory methods (LIFO, FIFO) and depreciation methods on financial statements. Additional procedures that are available for use in special situations include:

1.  Cash flow analysis—Cash flow analysis is especially useful in evaluating credit and investment decisions since it focuses on liquidity, solvency, and profitability relationships.

2.  Gross margin analysis—Gross margin analysis provides special insights into the operating performance of a company.

3.  Break-even analysis—Break-even analysis discloses relationships between revenue and patterns of cost behavior for fixed and variable expenses.

4.  Return-on-investment analysis—Return-on-investment analysis provides a comprehensive measure of financial performance.

These and other special tools of financial statement analysis are discussed later in this book.

**Time-series analysis** is used where data classified on the basis of intervals of time represent vital information in the control and operation of a business. The changes that can be isolated in time-series analysis represent the following major types of economic change:

1. Secular trend

2. Seasonal variations

3. Cyclical fluctuations

4. Random or erratic fluctuations

Special analytical procedures are available to isolate the different types of fluctuations as they relate to historical data and forecasts. When there is an established relationship between series, it is possible to use these relationships to make estimates and forecasts. Time-series analysis is not treated in this book.

**Regression analysis** is another tool of financial statement analysis. Regression analysis uses the relationship between a known variable and an unknown variable to estimate the unknown variable. **Correlation analysis** measures the degree of relationship between two or more variables. Regression and correlation analyses are more sophisticated techniques and are beyond the scope of this book.

## *SOURCES OF INFORMATION*

Statement users must often rely on statistics prepared by sources external to the company being analyzed. The following sources can provide additional information that can be used when analyzing financial statements:

1. Financial service organizations—Examples of financial service organizations include Moody's and Standard & Poor's, which give financial statistics, histories, and current developments for publicly reporting companies. These organizations do special studies on companies and industries.

2. Credit collecting organizations—Credit collecting organizations, such as Dun and Bradstreet, publish key business ratios for most industries.

3. Industry trade associations—Trade associations often compile industry statistics that can be useful for comparison purposes.

4. Investment and brokerage companies—Investment and brokerage companies often provide comparative statistics relating to individual companies, selected companies in an industry, or an entire industry.

A list of major sources of financial statement statistics is provided in the appendix to this book.

## SUMMARY

According to a committee of the Financial Analysts Federation, the elements of good reporting include:

1. Clear presentation of information that goes beyond the minimum reporting requirements and puts company operations in perspective.

2. Written commentary that explains why important developments occurred.

3. A timely, consistent, and responsible investor relations program that informs the financial analyst in an unbiased manner.

4. An ability to articulate and communicate the business philosophy and principal strategies of management and the way in which management is organized to carry them out.

Many analytical tools and techniques of financial statement analysis are available. In determining which ones to use, consider its relevance, controllability, consistency, comparability, and simplicity.

# Chapter 5

# ANALYSIS OF
# LIQUIDITY AND ACTIVITY

Short-term **liquidity** refers to the ability of a firm to meet its current obligations as they mature. Liquidity implies an ability to convert assets into cash or to obtain cash. **Short-term** refers to one year or the normal operating cycle of the business, whichever is longer. **Activity** refers to the efficiency with which a firm uses its current assets. In evaluating liquidity, analysts are interested in information relating to the amounts, timing, and certainty of a company's future cash flows.

Liquidity and certain areas of operating activity are dependent on the working capital position of a firm. **Working capital** is the excess of current assets over current liabilities. The amount of and changes in working capital from period to period are significant measures of a company's ability to pay its debts as they mature. Working capital is generated to a great extent through events that occur during the operating cycle of a business, including transactions involving investing in inventories, converting inventories through sales to receivables, collecting the receivables, and using the cash to pay current debts and to replace the inventory sold. Liquidity and activity ratios are useful in evaluating certain trends and relationships involving various aspects of the operating cycle of a business.

## LIQUIDITY RATIOS

The relationship of current assets to current liabilities is an important indicator of the degree to which a firm is liquid. Working capital and the components of working capital also provide measures of the liquidity of a firm. Ratios that directly measure a firm's liquidity provide clues about whether a firm can pay its maturing obligations. The current (or working capital) ratio and the acid-test (or quick) ratio are important ratios that are used to measure a firm's liquidity.

**CURRENT RATIO.** The **current ratio** expresses the relative relationship between current assets and current liabilities. The current ratio is computed as follows using data taken from the balance sheet of the Mythical Manufacturing Company, Exhibit 2.1:

$$\text{Current ratio} = \frac{\text{Current assets}}{\text{Current liabilities}}$$

$$= \frac{\$800,000}{\$340,000}$$

$$= 2.35 \text{ to } 1$$

It is convenient to set the computations in the following format:

|                     | 19X2      | 19X1      |
|---------------------|-----------|-----------|
| Current assets      | $800,000  | $760,000  |
| Current liabilities | 340,000   | 362,000   |
| Current ratio       | 2.35      | 2.10      |

The 19X2 ratio is interpreted to mean that there are $2.35 of current assets for each dollar of current liabilities. This represents an improvement over 19X1. A rule of thumb suggests that a 2:1 ratio is ordinarily satisfactory, but this is by no means a necessarily reliable relationship. Consideration must also be given to industry practices, the firm's operating cycle, and the mix of current assets. A very low current ratio would ordinarily be cause for concern because cash flow problems appear imminent. An excessively high current ratio could suggest that the firm is not managing its current assets properly.

**ACID-TEST RATIO.** A quick measure of the debt-paying ability of a company is referred to as the acid-test ratio or quick ratio. The **acid-test ratio** expresses the relationship of quick assets (cash, marketable securities, and accounts receivable) to current liabilities. Inventory and prepaid expenses are not considered quick assets because they may not be easily convertible into cash. The acid-test ratio is a more severe test of a company's short-term ability to pay debts than is the current ratio. A rule of thumb for the quick ratio is suggested as 1:1. Again, industry practices and the company's special operating circumstances must be considered. The 19X2 and 19X1 acid-test ratios of the Mythical Manufacturing Company are computed as follows:

$$19X2 \text{ acid-test ratio} = \frac{\text{Quick asset}}{\text{Current liabilities}}$$

$$= \frac{\$432,000}{\$340,000}$$

$$= \$1.3 \text{ to } 1$$

$$19X1 \text{ acid-test ratio} = \frac{\$384,000}{\$362,000}$$

$$= 1.06 \text{ to } 1$$

For each $1 of current liabilities in 19X2, there is $1.30 of quick assets available to pay the obligations. There has been a significant improvement in the quick ratio.

It is important to understand how various transactions affect particular ratios and working capital. Selected transactions will be used to demonstrate this issue. Assume that a company has an acid-test ratio of 2:1. The following transactions occurred, and their effect on the acid-test ratio and on working capital are shown:

|  |  | Acid Test Ratio | Working Capital |
|---|---|---|---|
| 1. | An account payable is paid in cash | + | 0 |
| 2. | An account receivable is collected | 0 | 0 |
| 3. | Inventory is purchased for cash | − | 0 |
| 4. | Inventory is purchased on account | − | 0 |
| 5. | A cash dividend is declared | − | − |
| 6. | Land is purchased for cash | − | − |
| 7. | Land is purchased for common stock | 0 | 0 |
| 8. | Marketable securities are sold for cash at a loss | − | − |
| 9. | Marketable securities are purchased for cash | 0 | 0 |
| 10. | Bonds are purchased for cash and held as long-term investment | − | − |
| 11. | Common stock is issued at a discount for cash | + | + |
| 12. | The cash dividend declared earlier is distributed | + | 0 |

The **cash ratio** is a more severe test of liquidity than the acid-test ratio. The cash ratio is computed by dividing cash by current liabilities.

**WORKING CAPITAL TURNOVER.** Working capital has a special relationship to sales, especially through accounts receivable, inventory, and cash. The ratio of sales to working capital can be used as a measure of the effectiveness of a company's use of working capital to generate sales. The working capital ratio is computed as follows:

$$\text{Working capital turnover} = \frac{\text{Net sales}}{\text{Average working capital}}$$

## ACTIVITY RATIOS

Activity ratios are used to evaluate a firm's operating cycle and the mix of its current assets. **Mix** refers to how quickly current assets can be converted into cash. Activity (or turnover) ratios can be computed for inventory, accounts receivable, and total assets.

**INVENTORY RATIOS.** The inventory turnover ratio establishes the relationship between the volume of goods sold and inventory. The inventory turnover for business in different industries and within industries can vary widely. A grocery store may have an average turnover of 20, for all items. A furniture store would normally have a much smaller turnover.

The inventory turnover is computed as follows, using the *average* inventory (where data are available) as the denominator because the ratio is intended to measure activity or turnover during the period.

$$\text{Inventory turnover} = \frac{\text{Cost of goods sold}}{\text{Average inventory}}$$

Average inventory is computed as follows: beginning of period inventory plus end of period inventory divided by two. If the beginning of the period inventory is not available, as in the 19X1 computation below, the end of the period inventory would be used in the denominator of the formula. When cost of goods sold is not available, some analysts use net sales in the numerator. The computation of the 19X2 and 19X1 inventory turnovers is shown here:

$$19X2 \text{ inventory turnover } = \frac{\$1,070,000}{\$365,000}$$

$$= 2.93$$

$$19X1 \text{ inventory turnover } = \frac{\$1,034,000}{\$370,000}$$

$$= 2.79$$

The turnover of 2.93 means that goods are bought and sold out more than 2.93 times per year on average. Generally, a high inventory turnover indicates that the firm (1) is operating effectively as far as inventory is concerned (purchasing, receiving, storing, selling), (2) investment in inventory is reduced, (3) the operating cycle in which inventory is converted to cash is shortened, and (4) less opportunity for the inventory to become obsolete exists. An excessively high inventory turnover may suggest that the company is not keeping sufficient inventory on hand to meet sales requirements resulting in stockouts and unhappy customers. A low value for the inventory turnover ratio suggests an excessive amount of inventory on hand, slow sales, high carrying costs for the inventory, and weak cash inflow prospects. A low turnover could increase the company's exposure to future financing problems. Intercompany comparisons of inventory turnover do not provide valid comparisons when the companies are using different inventory methods, e.g., FIFO and LIFO, since the cost of goods sold and inventory under LIFO during periods of rising prices will be higher and lower, respectively, than under FIFO.

To compute the number of days in ending inventory, the following formula is used:

$$\text{Number of days in ending inventory } = \frac{365, 360, 300, \text{ or } 250 \text{ days}}{\text{Inventory turnover}}$$

$$19X2 \text{ days in ending inventory } = \frac{360 \text{ days}}{2.93}$$

$$= 122.9 \text{ days}$$

$$19X1 \text{ days in ending inventory } = \frac{360 \text{ days}}{2.79}$$

$$= 129.0 \text{ days}$$

The number of days in ending inventory provides some idea of the age of the inventory and the days' supply in inventory. It also indicates whether a company is overstocking or understocking its inventory.

For analyzing the inventory of a manufacturing firm, additional ratios can be computed if the required data are available. The finished goods turnover indicates the liquidity of the finished goods, i.e., the number of times average inventory was sold during the period. The ratio could indicate whether a company was overstocked or understocked. The ratio is computed as follows:

$$\text{Finished goods turnover} = \frac{\text{Cost of goods sold}}{\text{Average finished goods inventory}}$$

A **raw material turnover ratio** indicates the number of times raw material inventory was used on the average during the period. The ratio is computed as follows:

$$\text{Raw material turnover} = \frac{\text{Cost of raw material used}}{\text{Average raw material inventory}}$$

A **work-in-process inventory turnover** can also be computed. This ratio is computed as follows:

$$\text{Work--in--process inventory turnover} = \frac{\text{Cost of goods manufactured}}{\text{Average work--in--process inventory}}$$

**ACCOUNTS RECEIVABLE RATIOS.** The accounts receivable turnover ratio expresses the relationship between credit sales and accounts receivable (and notes receivable if notes arise from normal sales).

Turnover refers to how often the average receivables were collected during the period. It is computed as follows, using net credit sales, where available, as the numerator since cash sales do not produce receivables, and average accounts receivable as the denominator:

$$\text{Accounts receivable turnover} = \frac{\text{Net credit sales}}{\text{Average accounts receivable}}$$

$$\text{19X2 ratio} = \frac{\$1,530,000}{\$301,000}$$

$$= 5.08$$

$$\text{19X1 ratio} = \frac{\$1,450,000}{\$290,000}$$

$$= 5.0$$

A high turnover ratio suggests that the receivables are being effectively managed, fewer resources are invested in receivables, and better credit and collection practices are in place. The number of days' sales in receivables for 19X2 is computed as follows:

$$\text{Collection period} = \frac{365, 360, \text{ or } 250 \text{ days}}{\text{Accounts receivable turnover}}$$

$$\text{19X2 collection period} = \frac{360}{5.08} = 70.9 \text{ days}$$

$$\text{19X1 collection period} = \frac{360}{5.0} = 72.0 \text{ days}$$

This computation gives a measure of the time the accounts receivable have been outstanding. An improvement is noted for this company. When the number of days' sales in receivables is compared with the company's credit terms (e.g., 2% 10 days, net 60 days), analysts can obtain some idea of how the company's credit and collection policies are working. This information also provides some idea of the age of the receivables. When this information is compared with the credit terms, with data for comparable firms in the same industry, and with prior years, the firm can obtain some information concerning the efficiency in collecting receivables and the trends in credit management.

**ASSET TURNOVER.** Asset turnover is a measure of how efficiently assets are used to produce sales. This ratio indicates the number of dollars in sales produced by each dollar invested in assets.

Generally, the higher the ratio, the more effectively the company has used its assets. This ratio is computed as follows:

$$\text{Asset turnover} = \frac{\text{Sales}}{\text{Average total assets}}$$

Long-term investments are usually excluded from total assets when they make no contribution to sales. If sales can be expressed in units sold, the ratio of units sold to total assets can provide basically the same information as the asset turnover except that units sold are not affected by price changes.

**ACCOUNTS PAYABLE RATIOS.** The relationship of accounts payable to purchases of the period can provide information concerning the proportion of payables outstanding. This ratio is computed as follows:

$$\text{Payables to purchases} = \frac{\text{Accounts payable}}{\text{Purchases}}$$

To compute the average daily purchases, the following formula is used:

$$\text{Average day's purchases} = \frac{\text{Purchases}}{\text{Days}}$$

To compute the day's purchases represented by payables, the following formula is used:

$$\text{Day's purchases in payables} = \frac{\text{Accounts payable}}{\text{Average day's purchases}}$$

The day's payable ratio is useful when compared to the credit terms given by suppliers. If the average day's payables is increasing, it could mean that trade credit is being used increasingly as a source of funds. If the company's payable period is less than the industry average, it could indicate that management is underusing available credit. If it exceeds the industry average, it could indicate that the company is overdue on its payables. Since purchase data are frequently not available to external analysts, an estimate of purchases is equal to cost of goods sold, adjusted for inventory changes. The analyst should also keep in mind that accounts payable reported on the balance sheet may not be limited to trade creditors but may include other payables.

## OPERATING CYCLE OF A BUSINESS

The company's operating cycle can be computed by adding the number of days' sales that are in receivables to the number of days in the company's inventory. In 19X2 and 19X1, the Mythical Manufacturing Company's operating cycles were 193.8 days (122.9 days in inventory and 70.9 days in receivables) and 201.0 (129.0 and 72.0), respectively. This can be interpreted to mean that the company's cash was tied up in inventory and receivables for about 193.8 days and 201.0 days in 19X2 and 19X1, respectively. A company with a short operating cycle typically requires only a small amount of working capital, reflected in relatively low current and quick ratios. A company with a long operating cycle typically requires a larger cushion of current assets and higher current and quick ratios, unless the firm's suppliers extend their credit terms. The operating cycle of a business is illustrated in Exhibit 5.1.

### Exhibit 5.1

### Normal Operating Cycle of a Business

| Cash | Purchases | Merchandise inventory | Sales | Accounts receivable |

Collection of receivables

## *OTHER CONSIDERATIONS*

Cash flow analysis should not be overlooked when evaluating the liquidity of a company. Especially useful cash flow ratios include:

- Current liabilities to cash flows
- Cash and cash equivalents to annual cash expenses
- Noncash income to total net income
- Cash flow to annual cash expenses

For additional cash-related ratios see Chapter 8.
These ratios are receiving increasing attention from analysts.

When analyzing the marketing function as it relates to operating performance, the management of a company could use the following ratios:

| Ratio | Interpretation |
|---|---|
| Sales/number of calls | Response per call |
| Travel expense/days | Cost awareness |
| Selling expenses/sales | Response per selling effort |
| Sales/sales orders | Sales efficiency |
| Number of calls/day | Sales effort |

These ratios are useful in developing trend information and an overall picture of the company's sales efforts. These ratios must be used with considerable care since they do not represent sophisticated marketing analysis techniques.

## SUMMARY

The liquidity and activity ratios provide information concerning the quality and liquidity of current assets, inventory, and receivables. Inventory and receivables usually constitute a major portion of a firm's current assets and working capital and must receive special attention when analyzing financial statements.

Creditors typically prefer companies with higher current and quick ratios and short operating cycles. However, excessively high ratios or short operating cycles could indicate unfavorable conditions. Analysts should be aware that companies sometimes "manage" working capital and ratios just before financial statements are presented to make working capital relationships look better than they are. This practice is commonly referred to as **window dressing**. Also, many firms follow an acceptable practice of using a natural business year that ends when inventories and receivables are lowest. Using the natural business year can make working capital and certain financial ratios more attractive than they might be if the company were using another accounting period, such as a calendar year. While the information derived from financial statement analysis can be extremely valuable, analysts should understand that financial statements have limitations and are compiled according to *accounting* assumptions, principles, procedures, and policies.

## QUICK SELF-STUDY

## PROBLEM I — Liquidity and Activity Ratios

The following data are available from the financial statement of a company:

| | | |
|---|---|---|
| Current assets | | |
| Cash | $25,000 | |
| Accounts receivable | 25,000 | |
| Inventory | 50,000 | $100,000 |
| Plant and equipment | | 500,000 |
| Current liabilities | | 50,000 |
| Long-term liabilities | | 200,000 |
| Sales | | 100,000 |
| Cost of goods sold | | 60,000 |

Compute the following ratios:
- a.  Current ratio
- b.  Acid-test ratio
- c.  Receivable turnover
- d.  Age of receivables
- e.  Inventory turnover
- f.  Day's supply in inventory

Your solutions:

a.

b.

c.

d.

e.

f.

# PROBLEM II — Multiple Choice

a.  Assuming stable business conditions, a decline in the number of days' sales in a company's accounts receivable at year-end from one year to the next might indicate

1.  A stiffening of the company's credit policies.
2.  That the second year's sales were made at lower prices than that of the first year's sales.
3.  A longer discount period and a more distant due date were extended to customers in the second period.
4.  A significant decrease in the volume of sales of the second year.

b.   In comparing the current ratios of two companies, why might it be incorrect to assume that the company with the higher current ratio is in a better financial position?

1.   A high current ratio might include large amounts of obsolete inventory.

2.   A high current ratio could indicate a company's inability to pay current debts as they mature.

3.   The current ratio includes long-term assets.

4.   The current ratio includes long-term debts.

c.   If a business enterprise has a current ratio of 3 to 1, which of the following transactions increases the ratio?

1.   Issuance of long-term bonds for cash.

2.   Borrowing cash on a nine-month note.

3.   Collecting a large amount of accounts receivable.

4.   Declaring a five percent stock dividend.

d.   Are the following included in the acid-test (quick) ratio? (Choose 1, 2, 3, or 4.)

|      | Accounts receivable | Inventories |
|------|---------------------|-------------|
| 1.   | No                  | No          |
| 2.   | No                  | Yes         |
| 3.   | Yes                 | No          |
| 4.   | Yes                 | Yes         |

e.   If current assets exceed current liabilities, payments to creditors on the last day of the month will

1.   Decrease current ratio.

2.   Increase current ratio.

3.   Decrease net working capital (assets minus liabilities).

4.   Increase net working capital.

# SOLUTIONS TO PROBLEMS

## Problem I

   a.  $100,000/$50,000 = 2

   b.  $50,000/$50,000 = 1

   c.  $100,000/$25,000 = 4

   d.  365/4 = 91 days

   e.  $60,000/$50,000 = 1.2

   f.  365/1.2 = 304 days

## Problem II

   a.  1

   b.  1

   c.  1

   d.  3

   e.  2. Note that a payment where the current ratio is less than 1 will decrease the ratio.

# Chapter 6

# PROFITABILITY ANALYSIS

Operating performance reflects the results of the profit-seeking activities of the enterprise. Much of the data required for evaluating operating performance is obtained directly from the income statement, which summarizes the results of operations. However, performance must be related to the assets that produce operating results. Furthermore, performance must be related to how outsiders (e.g., the stock market) perceive the performance and earnings of the enterprise. Some of the more significant ratios that relate to the evaluation of a company's performance and asset utilization will now be discussed. Dollar amounts used in the calculations are taken from exhibits in Chapter 3, which present the financial statements of the Mythical Manufacturing Company.

Profitability refers to the ability of a company to earn income. Net income is the single most significant measure of profitability. Investors and creditors have a great interest in evaluating the current and prospective profitability of an enterprise.

Profitability ratios have been developed to measure operational performance. The numerator of the ratios consists of profits according to a specified definition (gross margin, operating income, net income); the denominator represents a relevant investment base.

## PROFIT MARGIN ON SALES

Profit margin on sales indicates the dollar amount of net income the company receives from each dollar of sales. This ratio reflects the ability of the company to control costs and expenses in relation to sales. The formula for computing the profit margin on sales is as follows:

$$\text{Profit margin on sales} = \frac{\text{Net income}}{\text{Net sales}}$$

$$\text{19X2 profit margin} = \frac{\$95,500}{\$1,530,000}$$

$$= 6.2\%$$

$$\text{19X1 profit margin} = \frac{\$81,000}{\$1,450,000}$$

$$= 5.6\%$$

The profit margin on sales increased significantly from 19X1 to 19X2. The reasons for this change are related primarily to factors related to revenue and expenses reported on the income statement.

The net operating margin on sales ratio excludes nonoperating items, such as interest income and interest expense, gains and losses on disposal of discontinued operations, and extraordinary items. The net operating margin is computed as follows:

$$\text{Net operating margin} = \frac{\text{Operating income}}{\text{Net sales}}$$

The gross profit to sales ratio is helpful in evaluating operating performance and income. Gross profit is the difference between selling price (sales) and the actual cost of goods sold. This ratio indicates whether the company is maintaining or improving its markup on costs, which is a major business objective.

## RETURN ON INVESTMENT

Many analysts consider return on investment (ROI) one of the most important ratios for evaluating profitability because it relates earnings to investment. Return on investment can be computed on the following bases:

1.   Total assets
2.   Shareholders' equity
3.   Comprehensive basis

**RETURN ON TOTAL ASSETS.** The return on total assets or **total investment** indicates management's performance in using the firm's assets to produce income. There should be a reasonable return on funds committed to the enterprise. This return can be compared to alternative uses of the funds. As a measure of effectiveness, the higher the return, the better. The return on total assets is computed as follows:

$$\text{Return on total assets} = \frac{\text{Net income}}{\text{Average total assets}}$$

$$\text{19X2 ratio} = \frac{\$95,500}{\$1,324,000 + \$1,263,200/2}$$

$$= \frac{\$95,500}{\$1,293,600}$$

$$= 0.74$$

Interest expense net of income taxes is sometimes added back to net income in the numerator because the denominator includes the resources provided by both creditors and owners, hence the numerator should include the return on both.

**RETURN ON STOCKHOLDERS' EQUITY.** Return on stockholders' equity indicates management's success or failure at maximizing the return to stockholders based on their investment in the company. This ratio emphasizes the income yield in relationship to the amount invested. Financial leverage can be estimated by subtracting return on total assets from return on shareholders' equity. If the return on shareholders' equity is greater than the return on total assets, financial leverage is positive to the extent of the difference. If there is no debt, the two ratios would be the same. Return on stockholders' equity is computed as follows:

$$\text{Return on stockholders' equity} = \frac{\text{Net income}}{\text{Average stockholders' equity}}$$

$$\text{19X2 ratio} = \frac{95,500}{\$651,600}$$

$$= .15$$

$$\text{19X1 ratio} = \frac{\$81,000}{\$611,200}$$

$$= .13$$

Extraordinary items are usually excluded from net income in the numerator because such items are nonrecurring. Return on stockholders' equity is sometimes computed using the market value of the outstanding stock of the company instead of average stockholders' equity.

**COMPREHENSIVE RETURN ON INVESTMENT.** Return on investment is a comprehensive measure of financial performance. The ROI formula takes into account the major items that go into the balance sheet and income statement and so represents a comprehensive overview of performance. The relationship of ROI to balance sheet and income statement items is shown in Exhibit 6.1.

---

### Exhibit 6.1

### Return on Investment (ROI) Relationships

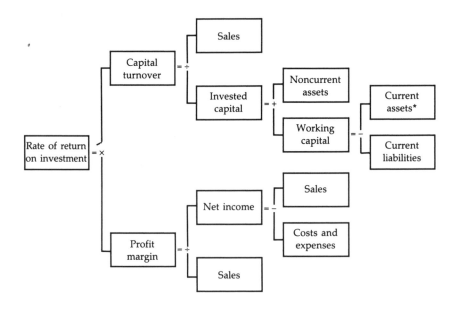

*Includes cash, accounts receivable, and inventory

---

The basic formula for computing a comprehensive return on investment involves the following components:

$$\text{ROI} = \text{CAPITAL TURNOVER} \times \text{PROFIT MARGIN}$$

$$= \frac{\text{Sales}}{\text{Capital employed}} \times \frac{\text{Net income}}{\text{Sales}}$$

Capital turnover is the ratio of sales to capital employed in generating the sales. Capital turnover is a measure of the use of assets in relation to sales. Generally, the larger the volume of sales that management can generate on a given investment in assets, the more efficient are its operations. **Capital employed** can be either (1) working capital (i.e., current assets minus current liabilities) or (2) total assets. **Profit margin** is the ratio of net income to sales and is a measure of operating efficiency. Return on investment can be improved by:

1. Improving operating efficiency (increasing profit margin).

2. Improving operating effectiveness (increasing capital turnover).

3. Using a combination of efficiency and effectiveness.

To illustrate the computation of ROI, assume the following information is available:

**Condensed income statement**

| | |
|---|---|
| Sales | $1,000,000 |
| Less: Costs and expenses | 800,000 |
| Net income | $ 200,000 |

**From the balance sheet**

| | |
|---|---|
| Working capital | $100,000 |
| Plant and equipment | 300,000 |
| Total assets (Capital employed) | $400,000 |

$$\text{ROI} = \frac{\text{Sales}}{\text{Capital employed}} \times \frac{\text{Net Income}}{\text{Sales}}$$

$$= \frac{\$1,000,000}{\$400,000} \times \frac{\$200,000}{\$1,000,000}$$

$$= \frac{\$200,000}{\$400,000}$$

$$= 50\%$$

Recall that the ROI formula can be restated as follows:

$$\text{ROI} = \text{Profit margin} \times \text{Capital turnover}$$
$$= 20\% \times 2.5$$
$$= 50\%$$

Various actions can be taken to improve the ROI, including the following:

1.   Increase total sales by increasing volume, sales price, or some combination thereof, while maintaining or improving the margin on sales.

2.   Decrease expenses, thereby increasing net income.

3.   Reduce the amount of capital employed (for example, reduce the inventory level, improve collection of accounts receivable) without decreasing sales.

If the chief executive officer of this firm wants to increase the ROI to 60 percent next year, and sales (price and/or volume) and invested capital cannot be changed, what change must occur in net income to achieve this objective?

$$\text{ROI} = 60\% = \frac{\$1,000,000}{\$400,000} \times \frac{\text{Net income (to be computed)}}{\$1,000,000}$$

$$60\% = \frac{\text{Net income}}{\$400,000}$$

$$\text{Net income} = \$240,000 \ (\text{i.e., } \$400,000 \times 60\%)$$

The comprehensive rate of return for the Mythical Manufacturing Company is computed as follows for 19X2; capital employed equals average total assets in this computation:

$$\text{ROI} = \frac{\$1,530,000}{\$1,293,600} \times \frac{\$95,500}{\$1,530,000}$$

$$= 0.74^*$$

*the same rate as computed earlier for the return on total assets

In this case, management must focus attention on profit margin rather than on capital turnover, which is assumed to be unchangeable. Since sales cannot be increased, the improvement in net income must come from a reduction of expenses.

Advantages claimed for ROI analysis include the following:

1. Focuses management's attention on earning the best return on total assets.

2. Serves as a measure of management's efficiency and effectiveness.

3. Integrates financial planning, budgeting, sales objectives, cost control, and profit-making activities.

4. Provides a basis for comparing companies.

5. Provides a motivational basis for management.

6. Identifies weaknesses in the utilization of assets.

An **investment (or asset) turnover ratio** can be computed by dividing net sales by average total assets for the period. This ratio also measures the effectiveness with which management used available resources in relation to sales. However, a situation could arise where this ratio was favorable in spite of a net loss being incurred by the company.

## *EARNINGS PER SHARE*

Earnings per share (EPS) data are widely used in judging the operating performance of a business. Earnings per share appears frequently in financial statements and business publications. It is perhaps the one most significant figure appearing on the income statement because it condenses into a single figure the data reflecting the current net income of the period in relation to the number of shares of stock outstanding. Separate earnings per share data must be shown for income from continuing operations and net income. Earnings per share may be reported for the results from discontinued operations, extraordinary items, or cumulative effects of changes in accounting principles if they are reported on the income statement. Current accounting practice requires that earnings per share be disclosed prominently on the face of the income statement.

If the capital structure of a corporation contains only common stock, earnings per share is computed as follows:

$$\frac{\text{Earnings per}}{\text{common share}} = \frac{\text{Net income}}{\text{Weighted number of common shares outstanding}}$$

If the capital structure contains common stock and nonconvertible, cumulative preferred stock or noncumulative preferred stock on which the dividends have been paid, the earnings per share is computed as follows:

$$\frac{\text{Earnings per}}{\text{common share}} = \frac{\text{Net income} - \text{Preferred stock dividends}}{\text{Weighted number of common shares outstanding}}$$

$$\text{19X2 EPS} = \frac{\$95,500 - \$700}{30,000}$$

$$= \$3.16$$

$$\text{19X1 EPS} = \frac{\$81,000 - \$700}{29,000}$$

$$= \$2.77$$

The **weighted average number of shares outstanding** in the denominator is equal to the number of common shares outstanding at the end of the accounting period if no shares have been issued or reacquired during the year. If shares have been issued or reacquired, a weighted average of these shares must be calculated. For example, if 10,000 shares were issued on July 1, these shares would be included in the denominator as 5,000 shares.

Corporations issue a variety of securities that can be converted into common stock—for example, convertible bonds and convertible preferred stock. Stock options and warrants are other securities that can be converted into common stock under specified conditions. If these common stock equivalents were converted, they would increase the number of shares of common stock outstanding and could decrease (dilute) earnings per share. If such securities exist, generally accepted accounting principles require a disclosure of the dilution that would develop if all possible contingencies occurred. In such cases, a dual presentation of earnings per share would usually be required:

1. Primary earnings per share—This presentation is based on the outstanding common shares and those securities that are in substance equivalent to common shares and have a diluting effect.

2. Fully diluted earnings per share—This is a pro forma presentation that affects the dilution of earnings per share that would have occurred if all contingent issuances of common stock that would individually reduce earnings per share had taken place at the beginning of the period.

The details of earnings-per-share computations are highly technical and are not a proper subject of this book. The basic factors entering into the computations of primary and fully diluted earnings per share are summarized here:

Primary earnings per share    =    Net income after taxes – preferred
dividends on noncommon stock equiva-
lents + interest and dividends (net of tax
effect) on securities considered to be
common stock equivalents
_____
Weighted average of common shares
outstanding + shares issuable from
common stock equivalents

Fully diluted earnings        =    The numerator for primary EPS + interest
per share                          and dividends (net of tax effect) on
securities assumed converted for fully
diluted purposes
_____
The denominator for primary EPS + all
other contingently issuable shares

In the formulas, common stock equivalents are securities that, in substance, can be considered common stock. These include convertible debt and preferred stock, stock options and warrants, and contingent shares. Securities that have an antidiluting (increase earnings or reduce loss) effect on primary earnings per share are excluded from the computations. In the numerator of the formula, the addition to net income for "adjustments for common stock equivalents" could include such items as the after-tax effect of interest on convertible bonds and dividends on the preferred stock that were subtracted in determining net income available to common stock that must be added back. The special treatment given to stock options could also result in increasing the numerator of the formula.

The formulas used to compute earnings per share figures include arbitrary and subjective assumptions that can detract from their usefulness. Excessive emphasis should not be given to this one ratio. Many analysts use the conservative fully diluted earnings-per-share data when evaluating per-share earnings. This may not represent the current situation or future expectations.

# MARKET RATIOS

The price/earnings and dividend yield ratios can be used to measure the relationship between the market value of shares and earnings or dividends. The dividends payout ratio can be used to evaluate the company's dividends policy.

The **price/earnings ratio** (P/E) or **multiple** reflects to some extent the growth potential of a company and the market's evaluation of the firm's earnings. The P/E ratio expresses what the market is willing to pay for the earnings of the firm, e.g., a 15:1 ratio indicates that the market is paying $15 for every $1 of the earnings. An increasing ratio is generally considered a favorable growth indicator, since stock prices generally reflect investors' expectations of future earnings of the firm. The formula for computing the P/E ratio is as follows:

$$\text{P/E ratio} = \frac{\text{Market price per common share}}{\text{Earnings per share}}$$

$$\text{19X2 ratio} = \frac{\$35 \text{ (assumed)}}{\$3.16}$$

$$= \$1.20$$

Dividends per share simply reports the dividends distributed per share of common stock. It is computed as follows:

$$\text{Dividends per common share} = \frac{\text{Dividends on common}}{\text{Number of common shares}}$$

$$\text{19X2 ratio} = \frac{\$36,000,000}{30,000,000}$$

$$= \$1.20$$

Dividends per share data for a number of years are of special interest to investors. Dividends per share can be used to compute the dividend yield.

Dividend yield is a measure of a common stockholder's total return for the period. The dividend yield is computed as follows:

$$\text{Dividend yield} = \frac{\text{Dividend per common share}}{\text{Market price per common share}}$$

$$\text{19X2 yield} = \frac{\$1.20}{\$35}$$

$$= 3.4\%$$

The **dividend payout ratio** indicates the income available to common stockholders that has been distributed as a dividend. This ratio reflects the dividend policy of the company and to some extent management's perceptions regarding the uncertainties associated with future earnings. The ratio is computed as follows:

$$\text{Dividend payout} = \frac{\text{Cash dividends on common}}{\text{Net income} - \text{Preferred dividends}}$$

$$\text{19X2 ratio} = \frac{\$36,000}{\$95,000 - \$700}$$

$$= 38\%$$

The dividend payout ratio can also be computed as the percentage of EPS that is distributed to common stockholders. In 19X2 this would be computed as follows:

$$\text{Dividend payout} = \frac{\text{Dividends per share on common}}{\text{Earnings per share}}$$

$$\text{19X2 ratio} = \frac{\$1.20}{\$3.16}$$

$$= 38\%$$

## *OTHER CONSIDERATIONS*

Additional ratios are available to evaluate specific areas of profitability-related factors. The **ratio of selling, general, and administrative expense to sales** provides some information concerning the effectiveness of cost control efforts undertaken by the company as well as management's efficiency of managing operating expenses in relationship to changing sales volumes. With continuing inflationary cost increases, this ratio should be carefully monitored. Generally, this ratio should decrease with an increasing sales volume. Trend analysis is particularly useful in identifying areas of strength or weakness; any significant fluctuations in the trend should be investigated. The **ratio of advertising to sales** is especially useful in evaluating consumer-oriented enterprises. Intercompany and industry comparisons are especially relevant in such situations.

Operating profit per unit of capacity or service, such as per room for hotels or per bed for hospitals, indicates the profitability of available physical resources and compares operations of different sizes. Productivity ratios attempt to measure both output and input in physical volumes, thus eliminating the impact of price changes. **Productivity ratios** are usually set up as follows:

$$\frac{\text{Output (physical goods or services quantified)}}{\text{Input (direct labor hours or machine hours)}}$$

Just as pension and lease obligations are an important part of balance sheet analysis, pension and lease-related expenses can be a significant factor when the income statement is being analyzed. Companies are providing increased disclosure regarding pensions and leases. This information needs to be carefully studied and analyzed in terms of the underlying accounting principles applied.

## SUMMARY

The analysis of profitability or earnings performance is a major concern to investors and creditors. The analysts should keep in mind that the amount of earnings is affected by the accounting principles and practices followed in compiling the statements. Analysts should be concerned not only with the amount of earnings and their relationships to other statement factors but also with the quality of those earnings.

## QUICK SELF-STUDY

# PROBLEM I — Ratios

The comparative balance sheet and income statement of the Horizon Company are shown here:

**Horizon Company**
**Statement of Financial Position**
**December 31, 19X0 and 19X1**

|  | 19X1 | 19X0 |
|---|---|---|
| Cash | $50,000 | $80,000 |
| Accounts receivable | 20,000 | 10,000 |
| Inventory | 30,000 | 20,000 |
| Plant and equipment (net) | 200,000 | 160,000 |
| Total assets | $300,000 | $270,000 |
| Current liabilities | $20,000 | $10,000 |
| Long-term liability, 6% bonds | 150,000 | 150,000 |
| Capital stock (1,300 shares) | 90,000 | 80,000 |
| Retained earnings | 40,000 | 30,000 |
| Total liabilities and equity | $300,000 | $270,000 |

**Horizon Company**
**Income Statement**
**For the Years Ended December 31, 19X0 and 19X1**

|  | 19X1 | 19X0 |
|---|---|---|
| Sales | $123,000 | $102,000 |
| Less: Sales returns and allowances | 3,000 | 2,000 |
| Net sales | 120,000 | 100,000 |
| Cost of goods sold | 48,000 | 40,000 |
| Gross margin | 72,000 | 60,000 |
| Operating expenses | 47,000 | 40,000 |
| Net income | $25,000 | $20,000 |

Compute the following ratios for the Horizon Company for 19X1 (solutions are available at the end of this chapter).

1.  Current ratio
2.  Acid-test ratio
3.  Receivables turnover
4.  Age of receivables
5.  Merchandise inventory turnover
6.  Net income to sales
7.  Operating ratio
8.  Return on total investment
9.  Return on total assets
10. Return on stockholders' equity
11. Comprehensive return on investment
12. Capital turnover
13. Earnings per share
14. Price/earnings ratio (market price of stock is $10 per share)
15. Dividends per share (dividends on common stock were $2,600)

Your solutions:

| | | |
|---|---|---|
| 1. _____ | 6. _____ | 11. _____ |
| 2. _____ | 7. _____ | 12. _____ |
| 3. _____ | 8. _____ | 13. _____ |
| 4. _____ | 9. _____ | 14. _____ |
| 5. _____ | 10. _____ | 15. _____ |

# PROBLEM II — Multiple Choice

1.  In evaluating the future profitability of a manufacturing company, investors will usually be least concerned with potential increases in:

    a.  Investments in plant assets
    b.  Sales volume
    c.  Gross profit
    d.  Current ratio

    Your solution  _____.

2. On December 3, 19X3, True, Inc. had 100,000 shares of $10 par value common stock issued and outstanding. Total stockholders' equity at December 32, 19X4, was $2,800,000. The net income for the year ended December 3, 19X4, was $800,000. During 19X4, the company paid $3 per share in dividends on its common stock. The quoted market price of its stock was $48 per share on December 31, 19X4. What was the price/earnings ratio on common stock for 19X4?

   a. 9.6 to 1
   b. 8.0 to 2
   c. 6.0 to 1
   d. 3.5 to 1

   Your solution _____.

3. How are dividends per share for common stock used in the calculation of the following?

   | | Dividend per share payout ratio | Earnings per share |
   |---|---|---|
   | a. | Denominator | Denominator |
   | b. | Denominator | Not used |
   | c. | Numerator | Not used |
   | d. | Numerator | Numerator |

   Your solution _____.

4. Which of the following is an appropriate computation for return on investment?

   a. Income divided by total assets.
   b. Income divided by sales.
   c. Sales divided by total assets.
   d. Sales divided by stockholders' equity.

   Your solution _____.

# PROBLEM III —
# Primary and Fully Diluted Earnings per Share

The Prince Company has 20,000 shares of common stock outstanding during 19X6. They also have 1,500 shares of 8%, $100 par preferred stock that was issued in 19X5 for $110 per share when the average Aa corporate bond yield was 10%. Each share of preferred is convertible into four shares of common stock. (Because the cash yield of 7.27%, i.e., 8% x $100/$110, is larger than 66 2/3% of the average Aa corporate bond yield on the date of issuance, the preferred stock is not considered a common stock equivalent when computing primary earnings per share. However, it is used when computing fully diluted earnings per share.) The company had $58,000 net income for the current year and paid the dividends on the preferred stock. Compute the primary earnings per share and the fully diluted earnings per share for the Prince Company.

Your solution:

# SOLUTIONS TO PROBLEMS

## Problem I

1.  $100,000/$20,000 = 5.0
2.  $70,000/$20,000 = 3.5
3.  $120,000/$15,000 = 8 times
4.  365/8 = 46 days
5.  $48,000/$25,000 = 1.9 times
6.  $25,000/$120,000 = 0.21 = 21%
7.  same as no. 6
8.  $25,000/$300,000 = .08
9.  same as no. 8
10. $25,000/$130,000 = .192
11. $120,000/$300,000 x $25,000/$120,000 = .08
12. $120,000/$300,000 = .4
13. $25,000/1,300 = .208
14. $10/.208 = 48.1
15. $2,600/1,300 shares = $2 per share

## Problem II—Multiple Choice

1.  d. Although important, the current ratio would usually not be as significant as the other items mentioned.
2.  c. $48/$8 = 6 to 1
3.  c. Dividends per share is used in the numerator of payout ratio and earnings per share is in the denominator.
4.  a.

## Problem III

|  | Primary Earnings Per Share | Fully Diluted Earnings Per Share |
|---|---|---|
| Net income | $58,000 | $58,000 |
| Less: Preferred dividends (8% x $100 x 1,500) | 12,000 | 0 |
| NUMERATOR | $70,000 | $58,000 |
| Common shares outstanding | 20,000 | 20,000 |
| Increase in common shares due to conversion of preferred stock (1,500 x 4) | 0 | 6,000 |
| DENOMINATOR | 20,000 | 26,000 |

Computation of earnings per share:

Primary: $70,000 / 20,000 = $3.50
Fully diluted: $58,000 / 26,000 = $2.23

# Chapter 7

# ANALYSIS OF CAPITAL STRUCTURE AND SOLVENCY

The capital structure of an enterprise consists of debt and equity funds. The sources and composition of the two types of capital determine to a considerable extent the financial stability and long-term solvency of the firm. Equity capital is risk capital, and the return on investment to an investor is subject to many uncertainties. Debt capital must be paid on a specified date, usually with interest, if the firm is to survive.

There is no ideal capital structure common to all firms. In general, a firm should not have a heavy amount of long-term debt and preferred stock in relation to common stock and retained earnings. Senior security holders should be well protected, and the common stock should not be burdened by excessive debt. A company's capitalization usually depends on the industry, the financial position of the company, and the philosophy of management. Generally, relatively stable industries, such as utilities, have a higher debt to equity structure than industrial companies.

Companies with only common stock capitalization can be attractive to both investors and creditors because there are no prior claims ahead of the common. However, long-term debt and preferred stock can provide *leverage* to a company's capital structure and can possibly enhance the return to the common stockholders.

## CAPITAL STRUCTURE RATIOS

The relationship of equity to total liabilities is an important measure of the capital structure of a business. As stockholders' equity increases in relation to total liabilities, the margin of protection to creditors increases, other things remaining unchanged. The enterprise is less vulnerable to declines in business or the economy, the cost of carrying debt is reduced, and the company should be able to meet its obligations more easily. The *equity to total liabilities ratio* is computed as follows using data from Chapter 3 financial statements:

$$\text{Equity to total liabilities} = \frac{\text{Shareholders' equity}}{\text{Total liabilities}}$$

$$\text{19X2 ratio} = \frac{\$692,000}{\$632,000}$$

$$= 1.09$$

$$\text{19X1 ratio} = \frac{\$611,200}{652,000}$$

$$= .937$$

This ratio provides a measure of the relative claims of the owners and creditors against the resources of the firm. A high value of the ratio shows that the claims of the owners are greater than those of the creditors. A high value is viewed by creditors as a favorable sign that the firm has a high degree of security.

The **debt to equity ratio** is the reciprocal of the equity to debt ratio. This ratio measures the amount of leverage used by a company. It measures the number of times the shareholders' capital has been leveraged by the use of debt. A highly leveraged company involves a substantial use of debt and a limited use of equity. Investors generally consider a higher debt to equity ratio favorable while creditors favor a lower ratio. This ratio is an indicator of creditors' risk. Generally, the higher the relative amount of debt in the capital structure of an enterprise, the larger the volatility of net earnings. The ratio is computed as follows:

$$\text{Debt to equity ratio} = \frac{\text{Total liabilities}}{\text{Shareholders' equity}}$$

$$\text{19X2 ratio} = \frac{\$632,000}{\$692,000}$$

$$= \; 91.3\%$$

$$\text{19X1 ratio} \; = \; \frac{\$652,000}{\$611,200}$$

$$= \; 1.07$$

## SHAREHOLDERS' EQUITY TO TOTAL ASSETS

The **shareholders' equity to total assets ratio** measures the proportion of the firm's assets that is provided or claimed by the shareholders. The ratio is a measure of the financial strength or weakness of the firm. If the shareholders' equity is a small proportion of total assets, the firm may be viewed as being financially weak, because the shareholders would be viewed as having a relatively small investment in the firm. On the other hand, a high ratio of shareholders' equity to assets can represent a relatively large degree of security for the firm, but it also indicates that the firm is not highly leveraged. The ratio is computed as follows:

$$\text{Equity to total assets} \; = \; \frac{\text{Shareholders' equity}}{\text{Total assets}}$$

$$\text{19X2 ratio} \; = \; \frac{\$692,000}{\$1,324,000}$$

$$= \; .523$$

$$\text{19X1 ratio} \; = \; \frac{\$611,200}{\$1,263,200}$$

$$= \; .484$$

## NUMBER OF TIMES INTEREST EARNED

The **number of times interest is earned ratio** is a measure of the debt position of a firm in relation to its earnings. This ratio emphasizes the importance of a company's covering total interest charges. The ratio indicates the company's ability to meet interest payments and the degree of safety available to creditors. Concern over the impact of interest expense differs as between companies, different stages of the business cycle, and stages of the life cycle of the business. The ratio is computed by dividing income before any charges for interest or income tax by the interest requirements for the period. This ratio uses in the numerator income before interest and income tax because this amount indicates the income available to cover interest. Income taxes are paid only after interest charges have been taken care of. The ratio is computed as follows:

$$\text{Times interest earned} = \frac{\text{Income before taxes and interest charges}}{\text{Interest charges}}$$

$$\text{19X2 ratio} = \frac{\$95,500 + \$41,500 + \$34,000}{\$34,000}$$

$$= 5.03$$

$$\text{19X1 ratio} = \frac{\$81,000 + \$44,000 + \$34,000}{\$34,000}$$

$$= 4.68$$

It appears that there is adequate coverage for the interest charges in this case.

## *LEVERAGE*

**Leverage** is used to explain a firm's ability to use fixed-cost assets or funds to magnify the returns to its owners. Leverage exists whenever a company has fixed costs. There are three types of leverage in financial management: operating, financial, and total leverage.

**Financial leverage** is a financing technique that uses borrowed funds or preferred stock (items involving fixed financial costs) to improve the return on an equity investment. As long as a higher rate of return can be earned on assets than is paid for the capital used to acquire the assets, the rate of return to owners can be increased. This is referred to as **positive financial leverage.** Financial leverage is used in many business transactions, especially where real estate and financing by bonds or preferred stock instead of common stock are involved. Financial leverage is concerned with the relationship between the firm's earnings before interest and taxes (EBIT) and the earnings available to common stockholders or other owners. Financial leverage is often referred to as "trading on the equity."

**Operating leverage** is based on the relationship between a firm's sales revenue and its earnings before interest and taxes. Operating leverage arises when an enterprise has a relatively large amount of fixed costs in its total costs.

**Total leverage** reflects the impact of operating and financial leverage on the total risk of the firm (the degree of uncertainty associated with the firm's ability to cover its fixed-payment obligations).

Financial leverage arises as a result of fixed financial charges related to the presence of bonds or preferred stock. Such charges do not vary with the firm's earnings before interest and taxes. The effect of financial leverage is that an increase in the firm's earnings before interest and taxes results in a greater than proportional increase in the firm's earnings per share. A decrease in the firm's earnings before interest and taxes results in a more than proportional decrease in the firm's earnings per share. The degree of financial leverage (DFL) can be measured by the following formula:

$$\text{Degree of financial leverage (DFL)} = \frac{\text{Percentage change in earnings per share}}{\text{Percentage change in earnings before interest and taxes}}$$

The degree of financial leverage indicates how large a change in earnings per share will result from a given percentage change in earnings before interest and taxes. Whenever the degree of financial leverage is greater than one, financial leverage exists. The higher this quotient, the larger the degree of financial leverage.

Operating leverage refers to the extent that fixed costs are utilized in the production process during an operating cycle. Operating leverage can also be used to measure the impact on earnings per share of having different levels of fixed to variable costs in manufacturing products. Earnings before interest and taxes are related to changes in the variable-cost-to-fixed-cost relationship. As fixed operating costs are added by the firm, the potential operating profits and losses are magnified and are ultimately reflected in the variation in earnings per share of stock. For example, a book publisher's cost of producing another book is below the average cost of producing the book; hence, the gross margin (sales less cost of goods sold) per book is relatively large. An enterprise with a large percentage increase in income relative to its increase in unit sales can expect to have large operating leverage. The degree of operating leverage (DOL) can be measured by the following:

$$\text{Degree of operating leverage (DOL)} = \frac{\text{Percentage change in earnings before interest and taxes}}{\text{Percentage change in sales}}$$

The degree of operating leverage indicates how large a change in operating profit will result from a given percentage change in sales. As long as the degree of operating leverage is greater than one, there is positive operating leverage.

Total leverage indicates a firm's ability to use both operating and financial fixed costs to magnify the effect of changes in sales on a firm's earnings per share. The degree of total or combined leverage (DTL) is computed as follows:

$$\text{Degree of total leverage (DTL)} = \frac{\text{Percentage change in earnings per share}}{\text{Percentage change in sales}}$$

Whenever the percentage change in earnings per share resulting from a given percentage change in sales exceeds the percentage change in sales, total leverage is positive. The total or combined leverage for a company equals the **product** of the operating and financial leverages (DTL = DOL × DFL).

Exhibit 7.1 illustrates the application of leverages to a firm's income statement. In this illustration, note that fixed expenses and interest expense remain unchanged. Note the section of the statement involved in the computation of operating leverage, financial leverage, and total leverage. Also note that what provides the leverage is fixed expenses and interest expense, which remain unchanged. When operating, financial, and total leverages increase, the risks the firm assumes also increase, since the total risk of the firm is related to the firm's ability to cover fixed operating and financial costs. In the illustration, note that the total or combined leverage of 2.0 is the result of multiplying 1.2 (DOL) by 1.67 (DFL). For this illustration, if sales increase by 1 percent, EBIT will increase by 1.2 percent. If EBIT increases by 10 percent, net income will increase by 18.7 percent. With total leverage of 2.0, in order to increase net income by 10 percent, sales must increase by 5 percent. Leverage analysis is an extension of breakeven analysis and uses the same basic information: price, quantity, variable expenses, and fixed expenses.

## BOOK VALUE PER SHARE

The book value (or equity) per share is usually computed at a price equal to the equity per share of the outstanding stock. The computation of book value per share is usually computed on the going-concern value of the enterprise, not on the liquidation value. The computation is made as follows:

## Exhibit 7.1

### Financial, Operating, and Total Leverage

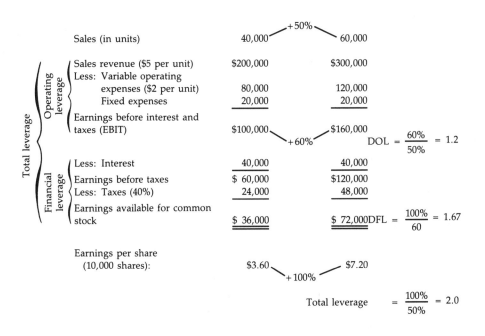

$$\text{Book value per common stock share} = \frac{\text{Common stockholders' equity}}{\text{Number of common shares outstanding}}$$

If a corporation has treasury stock, the balance in the treasury stock account is deducted to determine the common stockholders' equity. If a company has preferred stock outstanding, the total equity of the preferred stock must first be computed and deducted from total stockholders' equity to determine the amount of stockholders' equity belonging to the common shares. In the case of the Mythical Manufacturing company, there is preferred stock outstanding. In computing the equity of the preferred stock, any dividends in arrears must be assigned to the preferred stock, if it is cumulative preferred stock, along with either the (1) par or stated value, (2) call price, or (3) liquidation price of the preferred stock. The call price is frequently used if it is available because this represents the maximum claim to net assets available to the preferred shares. The book value per share of common stock for the Mythical Manufacturing Company is computed as follows for 19X2:

| | |
|---|---|
| Total stockholders' equity | $692,000,000 |
| Less: Amount assigned to preferred stock: 120,000 shares, $100 par value (no call price or liquidating price) | 12,000,000 |
| Equity applicable to common shares | $680,000,000 |
| Book value per common stock ($680,000,000/30,000,000 shares) | = $22.67 |

Significant changes in book value of common stock can result from transactions such as the conversion of convertible bonds or preferred stock, issuance or retirement of common shares, stock splits and reverse stock splits, and other events. The analysts should be aware of these possibilities.

Book value per share is a figure that represents what the shareholders would receive for their shares of ownership if the corporation were liquidated without gain or loss. This ratio sometimes is referred to as the liquidation value per share. In other words, if the corporate assets could be sold for exactly the value carried for them in the books, all liabilities settled, and the remaining cash distributed to shareholders, all shareholders should receive the book value of their stock holdings.

Caution must be exercised in interpreting the meaning of book value. It must be understood that market value per share is usually different from book value per share. Market value is influenced by a wide variety of factors that may not be reflected in book value. Book value is determined from a balance sheet that reflects the accounting principles and procedures used in preparing the statements. This makes intercompany comparison of book value practically impossible.

## *OTHER CONSIDERATIONS*

Certain cash flow ratios are useful in evaluating long-term solvency as well as liquidity. These ratios include:

- Cash flow to long-term debt
- Cash flow to interest expense
- Cash flow to net income
- Cash flow to fixed charges

- Cash-flow coverage of particular categories of debt and preferred stock, e.g., senior notes, bank loans, serial bonds.

The trends indicated by these and similar ratios are of particular importance and deserve attention.

## *SUMMARY*

The evaluation of the relative size of the different sources of funds of an enterprise is a major factor in determining the financial stability of the firm, including the risk of insolvency. As a source of funds, debt has both advantages and disadvantages, especially as it relates to leverage. Since most long-term debt involves interest, the importance of earnings coverage of those charges can be appreciated. Earnings are used as a measure of liquid resources that can be generated from operations. Analysts must constantly monitor the ratios related to financial structure and solvency so that changes in factors affecting these ratios will be detected.

## QUICK SELF-STUDY

# PROBLEM I — Book Value per Share

The stockholders' equity section of a balance sheet appears as follows:

---

### Stockholders' Equity

Contributed Capital
    Preferred Stock—$100 par value, 9% cumulative and
        nonparticipating, 2,000 shares authorized, issued
        and outstanding                                     $200,000
    Common Stock—$10 par value, 50,000 shares authorized
        issued, and outstanding                          500,000
    Paid-in Capital in Excess of Par Value, Common     200,000
    Total Contributed Capital                       900,000
    Retained Earnings                               100,000
Total Stockholders' Equity                     $1,000,000

---

Compute the book values per share of the preferred stock and common stock.

Your solution:

## PROBLEM II — Book Value per Share

Assume the same data as in Problem I except that the dividends on the preferred stock are two years in arrears. Compute the book values per share of the preferred stock and common stock.

Your solution:

# PROBLEM III — Capital Structure Ratios

Assume the following data taken from the balance sheet of a company:

| | |
|---|---|
| Current assets | $150,000 |
| Total assets | 210,250 |
| Current liabilities | 30,450 |
| Bonds payable | 45,000 |
| Total liabilities and stockholders' equity | $210,250 |

Compute the debt to equity, owners' equity to total assets, and creditors' equity to total assets ratios for this illustration.

Your solution:

# PROBLEM IV — Interest Coverage Ratios

The following data are taken from the financial statements of an industrial corporation:

|  | 19X2 | 19X1 |
|---|---|---|
| Sales | $12,500,000 | $9,600,000 |
| Interest costs | 191,400 | 154,800 |
| Income before taxes on income | 250,000 | 101,900 |
| Taxes on income | 8,000 | 36,000 |
| Net income | 242,000 | 137,000 |

Compute the interest coverage ratios for 19X2 and 19X1. Explain the significance of these ratios.

Your solution:

# SOLUTIONS TO PROBLEMS

## Problem I

Compute the equity associated with the common stock:

| | |
|---|---|
| Total stockholders' equity | $1,000,000 |
| Less equity allocated to preferred stock | 200,000 |
| Equity allocated to the common stock | $800,000 |

The book values of the two classes of stock are computed as follows:
Preferred stock: $200,000/2,000 shares = $100 per share
Common stock: $800,000/50,000 shares = $16 per share

## Problem II

Compute the equity associated with the common stock:

| | | |
|---|---|---|
| Total stockholders' equity | | $1,000,000 |
| Less: Par value of outstanding preferred stock | $200,000 | |
| Dividends in arrears ($200,000 x 9% x 2 years) | 36,000 | |
| Equity allocated to the preferred stock | | 236,000 |
| Equity allocated to the common stock | | $764,000 |

The book values of the two classes of stock are computed as follows:
Preferred stock: $236,000/2,000 shares = $118 per share
Common stock: $764,000/50,000 shares = $15.28 per share

## Problem III

The debt to equity ratio is computed as follows:

Total debt/Total owners' equity = $75,450/$134,800 = 56%.

The owners are providing more resources than the creditors. This is a widely used ratio which establishes the direct relationship between debt and owners' equity.

The owners' equity to total assets ratio is computed as follows:

Owners' equity / Total assets = $134,800 / $210,250 = 64%

This ratio measures the relationship between owners' equity and total assets. It represents the percentage of total resources provided by owners, including retained earnings. The owners provided 64% of the total assets, and creditors provided 36%.

The creditors' equity to total assets ratio is computed as follows:

Total debt / Total assets = 75,450 / $210,250 = 36%

Creditors have provided 36% of the total assets. Note that when the owners' equity to total assets ratio (64%) and the creditors' equity to total assets ratio (36%) are added, the total is 100%, as one might expect.

Ordinarily, the computation of only one of the three ratios computed in this problem would be necessary to measure the equity and debt position of a company.


## Problem IV

The interest coverage for 19X2 and 19X1 are computed as follows:

Net income before taxes + interest expense / interest expense
19X2: $250.0 + $191.4 / $191.4 = 2.31
19X1: $101.9 + $154.8 / $154.8 = 1.66

Net income before taxes is used because interest expense is tax deductible. This ratio improved from 1.66 to 2.31, primarily because of the increase in earnings in spite of the increase in interest expense. The ratios appear to be low and might indicate a problem.

# Chapter 8

# *THE CASH FLOWS STATEMENT*

Assessing the amounts, timing, and uncertainty of cash flows is one of the basic objectives of financial reporting. The statement that provides information needed to meet this objective is a statement of cash flows. The statement of cash flows presents a detailed summary of all the cash inflows and outflows, or the sources and uses of cash, during the period.

The Financial Accounting Standards Board issued *Statement of Financial Accounting Standards No. 95*, "Statement of Cash Flows" (November 1987), which requires that a statement of cash flows be reported as a basic financial statement when a business enterprise issues financial statements that report both financial position and results of operations. A statement of cash flows shall be presented for each accounting period for which results of operations are presented. The cash flows statement is prepared on a cash basis and not on the accrual basis of accounting, as are the balance sheet and the income statement.

The statement of cash flows helps users to see how the balance sheet of the entity has changed from the beginning of the accounting period to the end of the period. Exhibit 8.1 shows how the statement of cash flows fits in (articulates) with the other primary financial statements. The statement of cash flows uses the information shown in the other financial statements to disclose on one statement the causes of changes in cash during a reporting period.

## Exhibit 8.1

### Articulation of the Financial Statements

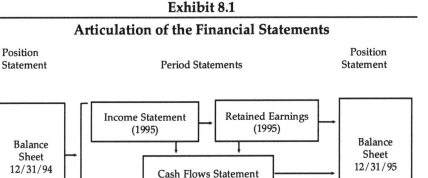


# *OBJECTIVES OF THE STATEMENT*

The statement's value is that it helps meet the informational needs of users including the needs for

1.  Liquidity—the nearness to cash of its assets and liabilities.

2.  Operating capability—the ability to maintain a given level of operations.

3.  Financial flexibility—the ability to take effective actions to alter the amount and timing of future cash flows so the company can respond to unexpected needs and opportunities.

The statement of cash flows can also help external users to assess

1.  A firm's ability to generate positive future cash flows.

2.  A firm's ability to meet its obligations and pay dividends.

3.  A firm's needs for external financing.

4.  The differences between a firm's net income and associated cash receipts and payments.

5.  The cash and noncash aspects of a firm's investing and financing transactions during the accounting period.

Generally, information about the gross amounts of cash receipts and cash payments during a period is more relevant than information about the net amounts. For example, investing and financing activities that provide both cash receipts and cash payments during an accounting period should be reported separately on the statements of cash flows. If a company issues new long-term debt to retire maturing debt, under financing activities the cash proceeds from the new issuances of long-term debt should be reported separately from cash payments for maturing debt issues. In certain cases where the turnover is quick, the amounts are large, and the maturities are short, net presentation is allowed in the statement of cash flows. An example would be the purchases and sales of short-term investments that are not cash equivalents.

Cash flows are important indicators of a firm's profitability and viability. Cash basis information provides critical support to accrual basis accounting (but does not replace the need for accrual basis accounting).

## CASH AND CASH EQUIVALENTS

In the cash flows statement, cash flows include "cash and cash equivalents." Cash equivalents are short-term highly liquid investments, such as treasury bills, commercial paper, money market funds, and, for an enterprise with banking operations, federal funds sold. They must be readily convertible to known amounts of cash and so near their maturity that they present insignificant risk of changes in value because of changes in interest rates. Generally, cash equivalents include only investments with original maturities of three months or less. An enterprise shall establish a policy concerning which of these investments shall be treated as cash equivalents and this policy shall be disclosed. A change to this policy is a change in accounting principle that shall be effected by restatement of all comparative financial statements presented. The total amounts of cash and cash equivalents at the beginning and end of the period shown in the statement of cash flows shall be the same amount as similarly titled line items or subtotals shown in the statement of financial position as of those dates.

## CONTENTS OF THE STATEMENT

The statement of cash flows reports cash flows relating to the operating, financing, and investing activities of a company.

1. Operating activities include all transactions and events that are not investing and financing activities. Such activities include revenues

and expense transactions associated with the sale of products or the delivery of services, e.g., all activities that enter into the determination of net income. Operating activities for a company could include cash flows from:

    a.   Cash inflows from selling of goods, providing of services, dividend income, interest income.

    b.   Cash outflows for inventory, salaries, tax expense, interest expense, and other expenses.

2.    Financing activities involve liability and owners' equity items and include:

    a.   Cash inflows from sales of capital stock and issuance of bonds, notes, mortgages, and other short-term and long-term borrowings.

    b.   Cash outflows for purchase of treasury stock, repayment of principal on borrowings, and cash dividends.

3.    Investing activities include:

    a.   Cash inflows from sale of plant assets and investment securities or collection of loans made by the entity.

    b.   Cash outflows for purchases of plant assets, purchase of investments or securities, and loans made by the entity.

In the statement, the inflows and outflows for each category should be shown separately, and the net cash flows (the difference between the inflows and outflows) should be reported.

The statement must also clearly show (1) the net increase or decrease in cash for the period and (2) a reconciliation of the beginning cash balance to the ending cash balance.

## *THE DIRECT AND INDIRECT METHODS*

*SFAS No. 95* allows two ways to calculate and report a company's cash from operating activities on its statement of cash flows. Cash flows from operating activities can be computed under either the direct method or the indirect method. The **direct method** shows cash receipts from revenues as compared with cash payments for expenses. When the direct method is used, the statement of cash flows reports cash inflows and outflows from operating activities as follows:

Cash inflows:

| | |
|---|---|
| Collections from customers | $900,000 |
| Interest and dividends collected | 20,000 |
| Other operating receipts | 9,000 |
| Cash inflows from operating activities | $929,000 |

Cash outflows:

| | |
|---|---|
| Payment to suppliers and employees | $600,000 |
| Payment of interest | 50,000 |
| Other operating payments | 50,000 |
| Payment of income taxes | 100,000 |
| Cash outflows from operating activities | $800,000 |
| Net cash flow from operating activities | $129,000 |

When the **indirect method** of reporting operating activities is used, net income is adjusted for items included in the income statement that do not result in an inflow or outflow of cash from operating activities. The effect is to eliminate from net income any noncash transaction to determine the net cash flow from operating activities. The indirect method provides a link between the statement of cash flows and the income statement and balance sheet. In effect, the indirect method is a reconciliation method. The indirect method of reporting net cash flow from operating activities is illustrated as follows:

| | |
|---|---|
| Net income | $100,000 |
| Adjustments for differences between income flows and cash flows from operating activities: | |
| Depreciation expense | 10,000 |
| Increase in accounts receivable | (4,000) |
| Decrease in inventory | 15,000 |
| Increase in accounts payable | 12,000 |
| Decrease in taxes payable | (3,000) |
| Amortization of bond premium | (1,000) |
| Net cash flow from operating activities | $129,000 |

The following diagram shows the more common adjustments that are made to net income to compute net cash flow from operating activities under the indirect method:

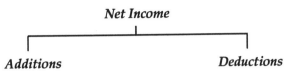

| Additions | Deductions |
|---|---|
| Depreciation expense | |
| Amortization of intangible assets | |
| Amortization of bond discount | Amortization of bond premium |
| Increase in deferred income tax liability | Decrease in deferred income-tax liability |
| Loss on investment in common stock using the equity method | Increase on investment in common stock using the equity method |
| Loss on sale of plant assets | Gain on sale of plant assets |
| Decrease in receivables | Increase in receivables |
| Decrease in inventories | Increase in inventories |
| Decrease in prepaid expense | Increase in prepaid expense |
| Increase in accounts payable | Decrease in accounts payable |
| Increase in accrued liabilities | Decrease in accrued liabilities |

=

*Net cash flow from operating activities*

To summarize the direct and indirect methods, when the indirect method is used for operating activities, net income reported on the income statement (from accrual basis income) is reconciled with the cash basis of accounting. When the direct method is used, revenues and expenses are converted from the accrual basis of accounting to the cash basis of accounting. The FASB prefers the direct method because it focuses directly on cash flows rather than the reconciliation of accrual net income to a cash basis description of operations—the direct method is considered more informative for this reason. Nevertheless, the more commonly used form of reporting cash flow from operations is the indirect method. If the indirect method is used, amounts of interest paid (net of amounts capitalized) and income taxes paid must be provided in related disclosures.

Regardless of whether the direct or the indirect method is used, the amount reported as net cash flow provided (used) from operating activities will be identical.

When the direct method is used, the preparer must present a reconciliation of net income to net cash flows from operating activities. This requires a separate schedule.

## SIGNIFICANT NONCASH TRANSACTIONS

Some significant noncash transactions and other events that are investing or financing activities are omitted from the body of the statement of cash flows. Such items are presented either in a separate schedule or in a narrative description and include the following: (1) the acquisition of assets by assuming liabilities through the issuance of equity securities; (2) exchanges of nonmonetary assets; (3) conversion of debt or preferred stock to common stock; (4) the issuance of equity securities to retire debt. Stock dividends, stock splits, and appropriations of retained earnings are generally not reported as significant noncash transactions.

## CASH FLOW PER SHARE

A cash-flow-per-share amount shall not be reported in the statement of cash flows. This avoids confusing cash flow per share with the significant-earnings-per-share amount reported in the income statement. Net income is generally a better measure of performance than cash flows. The statement of cash flows is not an alternative to the income statement.

## FOREIGN OPERATIONS

An entity with foreign operations shall use in its cash flows statement the reporting currency equivalent of local currency cash flows using the current exchange rate at the time of the cash flows. That is to say, a statement reporting in U.S. dollars shall first convert cash flows in other currencies to U.S. dollars for reporting purposes. The effect of exchange rate changes on cash balances held in local currencies shall be identified separately in the statement of cash flows and reported as part of the reconciliation of the change in cash and cash equivalents during the period.

## COMPREHENSIVE ILLUSTRATION

A comprehensive illustration of a cash flows statement is presented in Exhibit 8.2 using the direct method to compute cash flows from operating activities. Supporting schedules are provided showing (1) the reconciliation of net income and cash flows from operating activities and (2) significant noncash financing and investing activities.

## Exhibit 8.2

### Cash Flows Statement
### TRADING COMPANY
### Statement of Cash Flows
### For the Year Ended December 31, 19X5
### Increase (Decrease) in Cash and Cash Equivalents

| | | |
|---|---:|---:|
| Cash flows from operating activities: | | |
| Cash received from customers | $464,000 | |
| Cash paid to suppliers | (260,000) | |
| Cash paid to employees | (67,000) | |
| Cash paid for rent | (24,000) | |
| Cash paid for interest | (27,000) | |
| Cash paid for taxes | (16,000) | |
| Net cash provided by operating activities | | $70,000 |
| | | |
| Cash flows from investing activities: | | |
| Purchase of machinery | (122,000) | |
| Proceeds from disposal of machinery | 14,000 | |
| Net cash from financing activities | | (108,000) |
| | | |
| Cash flows from financing activities: | | |
| Proceeds from issuance of bonds | 210,000 | |
| Dividends paid | (8,000) | |
| Net cash from financing activities | | 202,000 |
| | | |
| Net increase in cash and cash equivalents | | $164,000 |
| Cash and cash equivalents at beginning of year | | 23,000 |
| Cash and cash equivalents at end of year | | $187,000 |

### Schedule 1
### Reconciliation of Net Income
### to Net Cash Provided by Operating Activities

| | | |
|---|---:|---:|
| Net income | | $34,000 |
| Adjustments to reconcile net income to net cash provided by operating activities: | | |
| Depreciation expense | $10,000 | |
| Decrease in accounts receivable | 44,000 | |
| Decrease in merchandise inventory | 9,000 | |
| Increase in accounts payable | 3,000 | |
| Loss on sale of machinery | 1,000 | |
| Amortization of premium on bonds payable | (1,000) | |
| Decrease in income taxes payable | (20,000) | |
| Decrease in interest payable | (10,000) | |
| Total adjustments | | 36,000 |
| Net cash provided by operating activities | | $70,000 |

### Schedule 2
### Noncash Investing and Financing Activities

| | |
|---|---:|
| Conversion of bonds payable into common stock | $138,000 |
| Notes payable issued for machinery acquired | $50,000 |

## FINANCIAL RATIO ANALYSIS

Cash flow ratios can assist in evaluating a company's financial performance in terms of strengths and weaknesses, financial management, investing policies, profitability, efficiency, cash sources, and cash adequacy. Cash flow data can be useful in predicting bankruptcy and financial distress. Developing benchmarks for each cash flow ratio in a particular industry can make the ratios more meaningful.

Useful ratios can be constructed from data on the statement of cash flows, the income statement, and the balance sheet:

1.   Quality of earnings (to support current level of operations and to generate future earnings):

   a.   Net income to cash provided by operating income:

$$\frac{\text{Net income}}{\text{Cash provided by operating activities}}$$

   b.   Reinvestment activities:

$$\frac{\text{Capital investments}}{\text{Depreciation + Proceeds from sale of assets}}$$

   c.   Cash flow for adequacy:

$$\frac{\text{Cash provided by operating activities}}{\text{Cash investments + Inventory additions + Dividends + Debt uses}}$$

2.   Financial management (reliance on outside financing for growth):

   a.   Cash provided by sources:

$$\frac{\text{Cash provided by operating activities}}{\text{Total sources of cash}}$$

$$\frac{\text{Cash provided by investing activities}}{\text{Total sources of cash}}$$

$$\frac{\text{Cash provided from financing activities}}{\text{Total sources of cash}}$$

   b.   Productivity ratio:

$$\frac{\text{Cash from operating activities}}{\text{Capital investments}}$$

   c.   Cash flow per share of outstanding common stock:

$$\frac{\text{Net increase in cash}}{\text{Number of common shares outstanding}}$$

3.  Mandatory cash flows (primarily interest and repayment of principal):

    a.  Long-term debt payment ratio:

$$\frac{\text{Cash applied to long–term debt}}{\text{Funds supplied by long–term debt}}$$

    b.  Total fund sources required for long-term debt:

$$\frac{\text{Cash applied to long–term debt}}{\text{Total cash sources}}$$

4.  Discretionary cash flows (e.g., for dividends, to acquire other companies, to invest in short-term securities):

    a.  Discretionary cash uses:

$$\frac{\text{Discretionary cash uses}}{\text{Total sources of cash}}$$

    b.  Individual discretionary use (e.g., dividends):

$$\frac{\text{Dividends}}{\text{Total discretionary uses}}$$

    c.  Dividend payout of cash from operating activities:

$$\frac{\text{Dividends}}{\text{Cash from operating activities}}$$

5.  Sufficiency ratios (adequacy of cash flows for meeting a company's needs):

    a.  Cash-flow adequacy:

$$\frac{\text{Cash from operations}}{\text{Long–term debt paid + purchases of assets + dividends paid}}$$

    b.  Long-term debt payments:

$$\frac{\text{Long–term debt payments}}{\text{Cash from operations}}$$

c.  Dividend payout:

$$\frac{\text{Dividends}}{\text{Cash from operations}}$$

d.  Reinvestment:

$$\frac{\text{Purchase of assets}}{\text{Cash from operations}}$$

e.  Debt coverage:

$$\frac{\text{Total debt}}{\text{Cash from operations}}$$

f.  Depreciation/amortization impact:

$$\frac{\text{Depreciation + amortization}}{\text{Cash from operations}}$$

6.  Efficiency ratios (how well a company generates cash flows relative both to other years and to other companies):

a.  Cash flows to sales:

$$\frac{\text{Cash from operations}}{\text{Sales}}$$

b.  Operations:

$$\frac{\text{Cash from operations}}{\text{Income from continuing operations}}$$

c.  Cash flow return on assets:

$$\frac{\text{Cash from operations}}{\text{Total assets}}$$

Notice that the cash flows from the operating activities classification on the statement of cash flows summarizes the cash effects of transactions and other events involved in determining net income. Operating activities are the company's primary activities. Cash flow from operations is a component of each of the sufficiency and efficiency ratios. The cash flow adequacy ratio measures a company's ability to generate cash to pay its long-term debt, reinvest in assets, and pay dividends. A value of 1 over several years would indicate the ability to cover these major cash requirements. The long-term debt payment, dividend payout, and reinvestment ratios when expressed as a percentage and added together show the percentage of cash from operations generally available for discretionary uses. The debt coverage ratio can suggest the payback period for the debt at the current level of cash from operations. The depreciation/amortization ratio indicates the percentage of cash from operations resulting from adding back depreciation and amortization. Some analysts would compare this ratio to the reinvestment ratio to give some insight into the sufficiency of a company's reinvestment and asset-maintenance base. This ratio can be used as an efficiency ratio. A company would be considered more efficient if depreciation and amortization had a relatively low effect on cash from operations. The efficiency ratios show relationships between cash and items appearing on the income statement, e.g., sales and income from continuing operations. The cash flow return on assets shows the return on assets on the basis of cash generated from total assets employed by the company.

## SUMMARY

Financial reporting provides information about how an enterprise obtains and spends cash, about its borrowing and repayment of borrowing, about its capital transactions, including cash dividends and other distributions of enterprise resources to owners, and about other factors that may affect an enterprise's liquidity or solvency. The statement of cash flows provides much of this financial information. The statement is currently required as an integral part of the financial statements.

The primary purpose of the statement of cash flows is to provide relevant information about a company's cash receipts and cash payments during an accounting period that can be useful in evaluating a company's operating, investing, and financing activities in a manner that reconciles the beginning and ending cash balances. Users of financial statements and financial statement analysts are duly concerned over the ability of the company to make cash payments to them in the future. Consequently, there is a major need for information about a company's activities on a cash basis.

Significant financial ratios can be computed and interpreted from items appearing on the cash flows statement. These ratios are of particular importance to investors, creditors, and managers.

## QUICK SELF-STUDY

# PROBLEM I — Questions

1. Mention several ways that the cash flows statement can be useful to a person when analyzing financial statements.

2. What information is provided on a statement of cash flows that cannot readily be obtained from other financial statements?

3. What is the meaning of "cash" as used in a statement of cash flows?

4. Which of the following items represents a potential decrease in cash?
   a. Goodwill amortization
   b. Sale of machinery at a loss
   c. Net loss from operations
   d. Declaration of a stock dividend

# PROBLEM II — True-False

1.  The statement of cash flows is not a required financial statement but may be presented along with other financial statements at the desire of management.

2.  The cash flows statement covers a period of time instead of a point in time.

3.  Investing activities reflecting a major section of a cash flows statement could include both cash inflows and cash outflows.

4.  Cash paid for interest is classified as operating cash outflow while cash paid for dividends is classified as an investing cash inflow.

5.  Cash flows from investing activities can be presented by either the direct or the indirect method of presentation.

Your solutions: True or False

1.  _____
2.  _____
3.  _____
4.  _____
5.  _____

# PROBLEM III — Multiple Choice

1.  Receipts from sales of property, plant, equipment, and other productive assets usually are classified as cash inflows from:

    a.  Operating activities
    b.  Financing activities
    c.  Investing activities
    d.  Noncash activities

    Your solution: _____

2.  Proceeds from the issuance of equity instruments should be classified as cash inflows from:

    a.  Operating activities
    b.  Investing activities
    c.  Financing activities
    d.  Lending activities

    Your solution: _____

3.  Which of the following items would be reported as a cash outflow
    from financing activities?

    a.  Payment to retire bonds payable
    b.  Interest paid on mortgage notes
    c.  Dividends payments
    d.  Collections from customers

    Your solution: _____


4.  A company purchased a three-month U.S. Treasury bill. What effect
    would this transaction have on a cash flows statement?

    a.  No effect
    b.  An outflow from financing activities
    c.  An outflow from investing activities
    d.  An outflow from lending activities

    Your solution: _____


5.  Which of the following should be reported when preparing a cash
    flows statement?

    |      | Conversion of long-term debt to common stock | Conversion of preferred stock to common stock |
    |------|---------------------------------------------|----------------------------------------------|
    | a.   | No  | No  |
    | b.   | No  | Yes |
    | c.   | Yes | Yes |
    | d.   | Yes | No  |

    Your solution: _____

## PROBLEM IV —
## Cash Flows from Operating Activities

The Blue Flower Company reported $200,000 of net income for 19X5. Items reported on the income statement included the following:

| | |
|---|---|
| Sales | $500,000 |
| Cost of sales | $200,000 |
| Salaries | $50,000 |
| Interest | $10,000 |
| Income taxes | $25,000 |
| Depreciation and amortization | $35,000 |

All sales were cash sales. The balance of inventory was unchanged during the year. Expenses requiring payment when incurred were paid in cash. Compute cash provided by operating activities during 19X5.

## PROBLEM V —
## Cash Provided by Operating Activities

The Ambition Company reported the following summarized data from its 19X5 income statement:

| | |
|---|---|
| Revenue | $100,000 |
| Expenses | 60,000 |
| Net income | $ 40,000 |

Accounts receivable increased by $15,000 during the year. Depreciation expense of $10,000 was included in the $60,000 expenses. Compute cash provided by operating activities for 19X5.

# PROBLEM VI —
# Cash Provided by Operating Activities

The following information is available from accounting records for the year ended December 31, 19X5:

| | |
|---|---|
| Cash received from customers | $400,000 |
| Rent received | 50,000 |
| Cash paid to suppliers and employees | 40,000 |
| Taxes paid | 40,000 |
| Interest paid | 20,000 |
| Cash dividends paid | 5,000 |

Net cash flow provided by operations for 19X5 was (show computations):

a. $355,000
b. $345,000
c. $350,000
d. $450,000

Your solution: ____

# PROBLEM VII — Cash Flows Ratios

Refer to the data in Exhibit 8.2, Cash Flows Statement for the Trading Company. The company has 100,000 shares of common stock outstanding. The company had sales of $1,000,000 and total assets of $1,164,000. Compute the following ratios associated with the cash flows statement:

1. One ratio to provide some information concerning the quality of the company's earnings for the period.

2. Two ratios related to financial management as reflected in operating activities and financing activities of the company.

3. Cash flow per share of common stock.

4. Dividend payout.

5. Reinvestment.

6. Depreciation/amortization.

7. Efficiency: (1) sales and (2) total assets.

# SOLUTIONS TO PROBLEMS

## Problem I

1. Answers will vary. The cash flows statement provides information about a company's cash receipts and cash payments, liquidity, and financial flexibility. It also provides details of the cash impact of its operating, financing, and investing activities. More specifically, it provides information relating to a company's ability to generate future cash flows, its ability to meet its obligations and to pay dividends, and the relationship between net income reported on the income statement and cash flows from operating activities as reported on the statement of cash flows.

2. The cash flows statement emphasizes the cash impact on assets, liabilities, and stockholders' equity from the company's operating, investing, and financing activities. It also shows details explaining the changes in cash flows during the period. It also reconciles net income as reported on the income statement with cash flows from operating activities. It discloses significant noncash financing and investing activities.

3. Cash includes "cash and cash equivalents." Cash equivalents are short-term highly liquid investments, such as commercial paper, Treasury bills, and money market funds.

4. c. Amortization does not affect cash flows. The sale of equipment results in an increase in cash. The declaration of a stock dividend does not involve cash. A net loss from operations suggests a potential decrease in cash in future periods.

## Problem II

1. False
2. True
3. True
4. True
5. False. The direct and indirect method are applicable only to the operating activities section.

## Problem III

1.   c

2.   c

3.   a, c

4.   a. The purchase of Treasury bills is a cash equivalent and therefore is not reported as an operating, investing, or financing activity.

5.   c. Both conversions are considered significant noncash financing activities and should be reported in a supplementary schedule.


## Problem IV

| | |
|---|---|
| Net income | $200,000 |
| Add: Noncash expenses (depreciation and amortization): | 35,000 |
| Net cash provided by operating activities | $235,000 |

Note that the sales and expenses other than depreciation and amortization involved cash. Therefore, the only adjustment required was to add back depreciation and amortization, which had reduced net income but which did not use cash.


## Problem V

| | | |
|---|---|---|
| Cash received from customers: | | |
| Total revenues | $100,000 | |
| Less: Increase in accounts receivable | 15,000 | $85,000 |
| Cash paid for expenses: | | |
| Total expenses | $60,000 | |
| Less: Depreciation expense | 10,000 | (50,000) |
| Net cash provided by operating activities | | $35,000 |

Note that the $15,000 accounts receivable outstanding at the end of the period were included in revenues but had not yet been converted into cash. Therefore, they had to be deducted from the total revenues. Likewise, depreciation expense was included in the $60,000 total expenses but did not use cash and so had to be deducted.

## Problem VI

c.  Dividends paid are financing activities and do not affect cash flows from operating activities.

## Problem VII

The ratios computed should be compared with prior years' ratios of the Trading Company, with the ratios of similar companies, and with the industry in which the company operates. The ratios could also be compared with budgeted ratios if they were available.

1.  $34,000/$70,000 = .423 (net income per cash from operating activities)

2.  a.  $70,000/$164,000 = .427 (cash per operations per net increase in cash)

    b.  $202,000/$164,000 = 1.23 (cash per financing activities per net increase in cash)

3.  $164,000/100,000 shares = $1.64 cash per share

4.  $8,000/$70,000 = .114 (dividend per dollar of cash from operations)

5.  $122,000/$70,000 = 1.74 (purchase of assets per dollar of cash from operations)

6.  $10,000/$70,000 = .143 (depreciation per dollar of cash from operating activities)

7.  a.  $70,000/$1,000,000 = .017 (cash per operations per dollar of sales)

    b.  $70,000/$1,164,000 = .06 (cash per operations per dollar of total assets)

# Chapter 9

# *INTERIM STATEMENTS AND SEGMENT ANALYSIS*

Companies frequently prepare income statements for stockholders and others. Such statements can provide a wealth of information for the serious investor. Also, many companies are required to disclose significant information about segments of their operations. Analysts should understand what kinds of information are disclosed in interim financial statements and segment reporting.

## *INTERIM FINANCIAL REPORTS*

Annual financial statements frequently encompass a time period longer than that required to permit timely reporting to investors and creditors of a company. Interim financial statements have been developed to provide a more timely source of information. Interim financial reports are frequently unaudited; if so, they should be clearly labeled "Unaudited" to avoid misleading the statement users. The statement analyst should understand what interim statements disclose and what the limitations of these reports are.

**Interim reports** are financial statements that cover periods of less than one year, such as a month or a quarter of a year. In general, the results of each interim period should be based on the generally accepted accounting principles and reporting practices used in the last annual reporting period, although certain modifications of accounting principles and practices are allowed when applied to interim reports. Interim reports are considered an integral part of the annual reporting period and are not viewed as discrete (independent) time periods.

Interim reports are essential in providing investors, creditors, and others with more timely information on the financial position and operating results of an enterprise. The usefulness of interim reports depends to a great extent on how they relate to the annual reports. Major uses and objectives of interim reporting include the following:

1.   To estimate annual earnings.

2.   To make projections and predictions.

3.   To identify turning points in operations and financial position.

4.   To evaluate management performance for a period of time shorter than a year.

5.   To supplement information presented in the annual report.

Accounting principles do not require as much information in interim reports as would be required in annual financial statements, although companies are encouraged to publish complete interim financial statements. Interim information is usually reported for the current interim period (e.g., the third quarter) and current year-to-date (e.g., January 1 to September 30 for a company reporting on a calendar year basis) with comparative data for the preceding fiscal year. Publicly traded companies usually report the following summarized financial information at interim dates:

1.   Gross revenues, provision for income taxes, extraordinary items, effects of accounting changes, and net income.

2.   Primary and fully diluted earnings-per-share data.

3.   Material seasonal variations of revenues, costs, and expenses.

4.   Contingent items, unusual or infrequently occurring items, and effects of the disposal of a segment of a business.

5.   Material changes in financial position.

Revenues are recognized in interim statements as they are on a report for a fiscal period. Product costs and other expenses are determined as they would be for the fiscal period, with some exceptions for inventory valuation, income taxes, and a few other items. The interim-period income tax is computed by applying the estimated annual effective tax rate to the year-to-date ordinary income or loss, and subtracting the previous interim year-to-date tax on the ordinary income or loss. Material contingencies that exist at an interim date must be disclosed in interim reports much as they are required to be when annual reports are presented. The contingencies are evaluated in relation to the annual report. Interim statements must disclose the seasonal nature of the activities of the company if such seasonal activities exist. Financial reporting for segments of a business is not required for interim reporting.

Analysts should understand that interim data are usually less reliable than annual data as a measure of a company's operations and financial position because of the shortness of the period. Also, disclosures on interim reports are usually very limited as compared with annual reports. Interim reports are also subject to management manipulation, especially by presenting conservative early quarter and strong ending quarter(s).

## SEGMENT REPORTING

Many U.S. companies operate in several different industries or in different geographical areas. When this occurs, the difficulties related to financial statement analysis are compounded. Investors who must evaluate the relative strengths and weaknesses of stocks of a diversified company have a difficult task when analyzing such companies if they report only the aggregate of their operations. Industry segments and geographical areas of operations can have different levels of risk and opportunity. Strengths and weaknesses of a company are difficult to isolate when only consolidated financial statements are presented and segments exist. For this reason, financial statement analysts prefer to rely on supplementary information provided in financial statements referred to as **segment reporting,** which provides disaggregated information to assist them in evaluating the company.

The need for segment information is the result of many environmental factors, including the growth of conglomerates, acquisitions, diversifications, and foreign activities of enterprises. Segment information is included (1) within the body of the financial statements, with supporting footnote disclosures, (2) entirely in the footnotes, or (3) in a separate schedule that is considered an integral part of the financial statements.

**REPORTABLE SEGMENTS.** A **segment** of a business is a part of an entity whose activities represent a major line of business or class of customer. A segment is a part of an enterprise that sells primarily to outsiders for a profit. Examples of a segment of a business include a subsidiary, a division, a department, a product, a market, or other separations where the activities, assets, liabilities, and operating income can be distinguished for operational and reporting purposes. Information about segments of a business, especially for diversified companies, is useful to investors of large, complex, heterogeneous, publicly traded enterprises in evaluating risks, earnings, growth cycles, profit characteristics, capital requirements, and return on investments that can differ among segments of a business.

A reportable segment is determined by:

1. Identifying the enterprise's products and services.

2. Grouping the products and services into industry segments.

3. Selecting the significant industry segments by applying various tests established for this purpose.

A significant industry is one which meets any one of the following criteria:

1. Its revenue is 10 percent or more of the combined revenue of all segments of the entity.

2. The absolute amount of its operating profit or loss is 10 percent or more of the greater, in absolute amount, of

   a. The combined operating profit of all industry segments of the entity that did not incur an operating loss, or

   b. The combined operating loss of all industry segments of the entity that did incur an operating loss.

3. Its identifiable assets are 10 percent or more of the combined identifiable assets of all industry segments of the entity.

**SEGMENT DISCLOSURES.** Segment information that must be disclosed in financial statements includes an enterprise's operations in different industries, foreign operations and export sales, and major customers. Detailed information must be disclosed relating to revenues, segment's operating profit or loss, identifiable assets, and other information. Segment information is primarily a disaggregation of the entity's basic financial statements. Publicly held corporations must report for **each reportable segment** of the entity the following information:

1. Revenues.

2. Operating profit or loss.

3. Identifiable assets.

4. Depreciation, depletion, and amortization expense.

5. Capital expenditures.

6. Effects of accounting changes.

7. Equity in net income and net assets of equity method investees whose operations are vertically integrated with the operations of

the segment, as well as the geographic areas in which those vertically integrated equity method investees operate.

Generally accepted accounting principles require companies to report the following items for each **foreign operation** if (1) revenue from such operations is 10 percent or more of the consolidated revenue or (2) identifiable assets of the entity's foreign operations are 10 percent or more of consolidated total assets:

1. Revenues

2. Operating profit or loss

3. Identifiable assets

If 10 percent or more of the revenue of an enterprise is obtained from sales to any **single customer,** that fact and the amount of revenue from each such customer must be disclosed.

Exhibit 9.1 illustrates segment reporting.

Segment analysis is especially useful in understanding the relative contribution of segments to the overall performance and asset base of a company. Segment information discloses a great deal about a company's diversification policy and enables the analysts to make meaningful industry comparisons. The analyst's task is made difficult because of the rather limited segment disclosures required and the accounting practices involved in compiling the data.

## SUMMARY

Interim financial statements can assist the analyst in determining trends and in identifying trouble areas before the annual reports are available. Interim reports usually contain more estimates than are found in the annual reports because of the tentative nature of the reports. This should be understood by the analysts.

In segment reporting, the required financial statement disclosures are basically a disaggregation of the company's regular financial statements. The same accounting principles are used for the segment data and for the financial statements, except that many intercompany transactions that are eliminated in consolidated financial statements are included in segmental reporting.

## Exhibit 9.1

### Interim Report
### Example Corporation
### Summary of Quarterly Earnings (Unaudited)

*For the year ended January 2, 19X2*
*(52 weeks)*

|  | First Quarter | Second Quarter | Third Quarter | Fourth Quarter |
|---|---|---|---|---|
| Net sales | $12,837,000 | $16,394,000 | $17,888,000 | $14,970,000 |
| Gross profit | 1,054,000 | 2,716,000 | 3,076,000 | 2,053,000 |
| Earnings (loss) from continuing operations | (125,000) | 579,000 | 896,000 | 458,000 |
| Earnings (loss) from discontinued operations | (26,000) | (33,000) | (33,000) | 13,000 |
| Net earnings (loss) | (151,000) | 546,000 | 863,000 | 471,000 |
| Earnings (loss) per share: |  |  |  |  |
| Earnings (loss) from continuing operations | $(.05) | $.24 | $.38 | $.20 |
| Earnings (loss) from discontinued operations | (0.1) | (0.1) | (0.1) | - |
| Net earnings (loss) | (.06) | .23 | .37 | .20 |

*For the year ended January 31, 19X1*
*(53 weeks)*

|  | First Quarter | Second Quarter | Third Quarter | Fourth Quarter |
|---|---|---|---|---|
| Net sales | $13,585,000 | $16,713,000 | $17,771,000 | $15,076,000 |
| Gross profit | 1,467,000 | 2,227,000 | 1,774,000 | 1,772,000 |
| Earnings from continuing operations | 228,000 | 654,000 | 570,000 | - |
| Earnings (loss) from discontinued operations | 281,000 | (11,000) | 15,000 | 31,000 |
| Earnings before extraordinary gain | 509,000 | 643,000 | 585,000 | 31,000 |
| Extraordinary gain | - | - | 1,834,000 | 1,655,000 |
| Net earnings | 509,000 | 643,000 | 2,419,000 | 1,686,000 |
| Earnings per share: |  |  |  |  |
| Earnings from continuing operations | $.10 | $.29 | $.24 | $- |
| Earnings (loss) from discontinued operations | .12 | (.01) | - | .02 |
| Earnings before extraordinary gain | .22 | .28 | .24 | .02 |
| Extraordinary gain | - | - | .79 | .71 |
| Net earnings | .22 | .28 | 1.03 | .73 |

# Chapter 10

# CONSTANT DOLLAR
# AND CURRENT VALUE
# ACCOUNTING

Conventional accounting requires that transactions should be recorded at historical cost. Users of financial statements are aware that historical cost financial statements have major limitations. During periods of inflation and deflation, historical cost statements cause distortions in financial statement analysis because cost figures of prior years are not comparable to current amounts reported. Various procedures have been suggested to deal with this problem. One procedure requires adjustments of accounting data for changes in the purchasing power of the dollar. This procedure is referred to as **constant dollar accounting** or **general price-level accounting.** A second approach to the problem of changing prices is current cost accounting. The **current cost accounting model** is designed to measure the change in the specific prices, especially for inventory, property, plant, and equipment. Analysts should be familiar with these techniques in order to avoid distortions due to general and specific price-level changes.

*FASB Statement No. 33,* "Financial Reporting and Changing Prices," as amended in 1985, describes inflation accounting requirements. Generally accepted accounting principles require certain large, publicly held companies to supplement their annual financial statements with information about the effect of changing prices on income from continuing operations and several assets, primarily property, plant, equipment, and inventory, and their related expenses. Statement No. 89 removed the requirement to present general purchasing power and current cost/constant dollar supplement statements; however, supplementary disclosures are encouraged.

## CONSTANT DOLLAR ACCOUNTING

**Constant dollar accounting** is a method of reporting financial statement elements in dollars that have the same (i.e., constant) general purchasing power. Constant dollar accounting is also referred to as **general price-level accounting.**

In constant dollar accounting, the dollars (not the accounting principles and methods) used in historical cost financial statements are adjusted for changes in the purchasing power of the dollar. These adjustments make it possible to compare dollar amounts from different accounting periods in dollars of equal purchasing power. Constant dollar accounting eliminates the impact of general inflation from the financial statements. The statements are restated using an index of the general price level such as the Consumer Price Index for all Urban Consumers (CPI-U). A price index is a weighted-average relation between money and a given set of goods and services.

The restatement of the financial statements amounts is done according to the following formula:

$$\begin{array}{c}\text{Historical cost of non--} \\ \text{monetary assets or} \\ \text{nominal amount of liability}\end{array} \times \dfrac{\text{Index at end of current period}}{\text{Index at date of nonmonetary transaction}}$$

$$\text{or } \$100{,}000 \ \times \dfrac{1996 \text{ index}}{1979 \text{ index}} = \text{Cost of item in terms of 1996 dollars}$$

where the cost of an asset acquired in 1979 is restated in terms of 1996 dollars.

In constant dollar accounting, an important distinction is made between monetary items and nonmonetary items. **Monetary items** are assets, liabilities, and equities whose balances are fixed in terms of numbers of dollars regardless of changes in the general price level, such as cash, receivables, and payables. All other items are **nonmonetary items,** such as inventory, property, plant, and equipment. In periods of changing prices, purchasing power gains or losses result from holding monetary items. For example, if one holds $1,000 in cash for a year during a period of inflation, purchasing power of cash is reduced at the end of the year. The difference between a company's monetary assets and its monetary liabilities and equities is referred to as the **net monetary position.** The relationship between a net monetary position and rising/declining prices on purchasing power gains and losses is illustrated here:

| | Rising prices | Falling prices |
|---|---|---|
| Monetary assets exceed monetary liabilities | Loss | Gain |
| Monetary liabilities exceed monetary assets | Gain | Loss |

The extent of the impact of inflation on purchasing power gains and losses depends on the amount of inflation that has occurred, the length of time that the monetary items have been held, and the mix of monetary and nonmonetary accounts. Net monetary gains and losses represent measurable gains and losses to shareholders and should not be ignored in analyzing a company. The computation of the purchasing power gain or loss on net monetary items is illustrated in Exhibit 10.1.

## Exhibit 10.1

### Computing Purchasing Power Gain and Loss on Net Monetary Assets

| | (000s) | | |
|---|---|---|---|
| | Nominal Dollars | Conversion Factor | Average 19X9 Dollars |
| Balance, January 1, 19X9 | $55,000 | × 220.9 (avg. 19X9) 212.9 (Dec. 19X8) | C$57,067 |
| Increase in net monetary liabilities during the year | 6,000 | | 6,000 |
| | | | 63,067 |
| Balance, December 31, 19X9 | $61,000 | × 220.9 (avg. 19X9) 243.5 (Dec. 19X9) | 55,338 |
| Purchasing power gain on net monetary items | | | C$ 7,729 |

*Assumed to be in average 19X9 dollars. (FASB 33, ¶232)

Source: FASB, Statement No. 33.

Constant dollar accounting provides for the meaningful comparisons of accounting data with measuring units that are comparable. For example, the sales dollars of the last period will have the same purchasing power as the sales dollars of the current period. Constant dollar accounting takes into consideration changes in the general price level. The recognition of the purchasing power gains and losses provides significant information concerning the impact of inflation on a company. For these and other reasons, proponents of constant dollar accounting maintain that constant dollar information is relevant to decision makers.

Constant dollar accounting does not take into consideration changes in specific prices of goods, such as inventories, plant, and equipment. Furthermore, constant dollar accounting requires the use of price indexes that can have statistical weaknesses, which could affect the reliability of the output of constant dollar adjustments.

The effects of general price-level changes can vary from firm to firm. Firms with a large proportion of debt will often have a large monetary gain from holding the monetary liabilities. This could be interpreted as positive in that such debts will be paid off eventually with dollars having less purchasing power.

Several studies indicate that for many companies when constant dollar accounting is used:

1. Income from operations, excluding purchasing power gain or loss, will decrease due to price-level-adjusted depreciation expense, which typically will increase, and the effect of holding inventories during periods of inflation.

2. Tax rates will increase significantly.

3. Rates of return on stockholders' equity will decline as a result of the decline in earnings and the increase in equity resulting from the impact of adjustments to inventory and productive assets.

4. Debt-to-equity ratios will improve, primarily because of the increase in equity.

## CURRENT VALUE ACCOUNTING

Accountants generally recognize that earnings result only after capital has been maintained or costs recovered. In this context, capital ordinarily refers to shareholders' equity or net assets of a business enterprise. Capital at the beginning of a period is maintained during the period if earnings for the period equal or exceed dividends (withdrawals) for the period. Earnings in excess of dividends for a period become part of investment capital or net assets to be maintained in the following period. There are two major views concerning the kind of capital to be maintained:

1.  Financial capital maintenance—dollars invested directly by owners or through nondistribution of earnings in the past. Financial capital maintenance can compute income measurement in terms of (1) historical cost or (2) current cost. Under financial capital maintenance, earnings occur if a company recovers more from revenues than the nominal dollars invested in the asset sold. This concept is associated with the conventional accounting and reporting system.

2.  Physical capital maintenance—physical properties of assets required to produce goods or services or productive capacity. Income arises only if an enterprise recovers in revenues more than the replacement cost of items sold.

The major difference between these two concepts involves certain changes in prices of assets during accounting periods that result in "holding gains and losses." **Holding gains and losses** are amounts that arise solely because of price or value changes in assets. For example, assume that an item of inventory is purchased on January 1 for $10,000 and its price on December 31 is $12,000. The asset is unsold at the end of the year. A holding gain of $2,000 resulted from holding the asset. The decision paths that result from the different views of capital can be diagramed as follows:

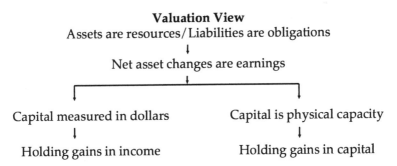

**Valuation View**
Assets are resources/Liabilities are obligations
↓
Net asset changes are earnings
↓

| | |
|---|---|
| Capital measured in dollars | Capital is physical capacity |
| ↓ | ↓ |
| Holding gains in income | Holding gains in capital |

The two capital maintenance concepts can be illustrated by a simple example. Assume the following:

Initial capital of $15,000 cash is invested in inventory costing $8,000 and a lathe priced at $7,000. The lathe has a 10-year life that will be depreciated using straight-line depreciation.

Inventory transactions during the year are as follows:
Inventory purchased as described above                                        $8,000
Inventory sold for $9,000; replacement cost
   at time of sale (inventory not replaced at this time)                       8,300
Actual cost to replenish stock                                                 8,500
Year-end inventory replacement cost                                            8,700

Exhibit 10.2 shows an income statement and a balance sheet assuming financial capital maintenance (at historical cost and current value) and physical capital maintenance.

Under the **historical cost concept of financial capital maintenance,** the company maintained its beginning-of-the-year $15,000 capital and earned $300 in income during the year. Accountants have generally used the concept of maintenance of financial capital based on historical cost because investors are assumed to be interested primarily in the monetary (dollar) return on their investment. Holding gains are not recognized until assets are sold. When holding gains are realized, they are not identified separately on the income statement.

Under the **current value concept of financial capital maintenance,** inventory and depreciable assets are revalued every year at current cost, usually replacement cost. Holding gains are considered to be income but are identified separately in the income statement.

Under the financial capital maintenance approach, holding gains and losses are included in income (or loss).

Under the **physical capital maintenance concept,** the cost of capital consumed (inventories sold and depreciation of assets) exceeded revenues by $90. Physical capital was not maintained. Notice that an additional charge must be made against income for the additional cost of sales and depreciation necessary to reflect those higher replacement costs. In the illustration, physical capital was eroded. Holding gains or losses are not reported on the income statement but are shown as separate components of capital on the balance sheet.

It is also possible to adjust current capital to reflect changes in the purchasing power of the dollar resulting from inflation or deflation. This is referred to as **current cost/constant dollar accounting.** Income is then shown after maintenance of the purchasing power of the investors' capital. Income results only if the company can recover from revenues more than the general purchasing power equivalent of its investment. The basic concept of capital maintenance is not changed as a result of this additional consideration.

## Exhibit 10.2

### Theories of Capital Maintenance—
### Financial Capital and Physical Capital

|  | Financial Capital | | Current Value/ Physical Capital |
|---|---|---|---|
|  | Historical Cost | Current Value |  |
| **INCOME STATEMENT** | | | |
| Sales | $9,000 | $9,000 | $9,000 |
| Cost of sales | 8,000 | 8,300 | 8,300 |
| Depreciation | 700 | 790 | 790 |
|  | 8,700 | 9,090 | 9,090 |
|  | 300 | ( 90) | ( 90) |
| Holding gains (inv. sold $300; inv. held $200; lathe $900) | — | 1,400 | — |
| Income (loss) | $ 300 | $ 1,310 | $ ( 90) |
| **BALANCE SHEET** | | | |
| Cash | $ 500 | $ 500 | $ 500 |
| Inventory | 8,500 | 8,700 | 8,700 |
| Lathe-net | 6,300 | 7,110 | 7,100 |
| Total | $15,300 | $16,310 | $16,310 |
| Capital | $15,000 | $15,000 | $15,000 |
| Undistributed income (loss) | 300 | 1,310 | ( 90) |
| Capital maintenance | — | — | 1,400 |
| Total | $15,300 | $16,310 | $16,310 |

Constant dollar and current value disclosures are relevant to investors and creditors who must assess cash flows, operating performance, operating capability, and purchasing power gain or loss resulting from changes in the general price level. Disclosures related to price changes can give statement users insights into how a company is doing in "real" terms.

## *SUMMARY*

Analysts are uncertain whether historical cost, historical cost/constant dollars, current cost, or current cost/constant dollar data are most useful for decision making. Financial statement disclosures that provide any or all of these data should assist the analysts in improving investment and credit-granting decisions. Financial statements adjusted for changing prices tend to confuse many financial statement users; further research and education are required in this area of reporting and analysis.

# Chapter 11

# SPECIAL SITUATIONS

Analysts sometimes encounter special situations with which they must deal. Several of these situations will be discussed in this chapter including the following:

1. Personal financial statements.
2. Development stage companies.
3. Companies in financial distress.
4. Business combinations.
5. Foreign transactions and operations.
6. Related-party transactions.
7. Subsequent events.
8. Fraudulent financial reporting.

## PERSONAL FINANCIAL STATEMENTS

The reporting entity of personal financial statements is an individual, a husband and wife, or a group of related individuals. Personal financial statements should provide adequate disclosure of relevant information relating to the financial affairs of an individual reporting entity.

For each reporting entity, a **statement of financial position** (or balance sheet) is a required statement. The statement of financial position is now required to present estimated current values of assets and liabilities, a provision for estimated taxes, and net worth. A provision should also be made for estimated income taxes on the differences between the estimated current values of assets, the estimated current amounts of liabilities, and their respective tax bases. Comparative statements for one or more periods should be presented. A statement of changes in net worth is optional. Such a statement would disclose the major sources of increases and decreases in net worth. Increases in personal net worth arise from income, increases in estimated current value of assets, decreases in estimated current amount of liabilities, and decreases in the provision for estimated income taxes. Decreases in personal net worth arise from expenses, decreases in estimated current value of assets, increases in estimated current amount of liabilities, and increases in the provision for income taxes.

Personal financial statements should be presented on the accrual basis and not on the cash basis. A classified balance sheet is not used. Assets and liabilities are presented in the order of their liquidity and maturity, respectively. A business interest that constitutes a large part of an individuals's total assets should be shown separate from other assets. Such an interest would be presented as a net amount and not as a pro rata allocation of the business's assets and liabilities. An illustration of a personal financial statement is shown in Exhibit 11.1.

## DEVELOPMENT STAGE COMPANIES

An enterprise is a **development stage company** if substantially all of its efforts are devoted to establishing a new business and either of the following is present:

1.  Principal operations have not begun.

2.  Principal operations have begun but revenue produced is insignificant.

Activities of a development stage enterprise frequently include financial planning, raising capital, research and development, personnel recruiting and training, and market development.

A development stage enterprise must follow generally accepted accounting principles applicable to operating enterprises in the preparation of its financial statements. In its balance sheet, the company must report cumulative net losses separately in the equity section. In its income statement it must report cumulative revenues and expenses from the inception of the enterprise. In its statement of changes in financial position, it must report cumulative sources and uses of funds from the inception of the enterprise. Its statement of stockholders' equity should include the number of shares issued and the date of their issuance as well as the dollar amounts received

## Exhibit 11.1

### Personal Financial Statement

### John and Mary Doe
### Statement of Financial Condition
### December 31, 19X3 and 19X4

| *Assets* | **19X4** | **19X3** |
|---|---|---|
| Cash | $5,000 | $3,000 |
| Investments | | |
| Marketable securities (Note 1) | 20,000 | 17,000 |
| Clix, Inc., a closely held corporation | 100,000 | 80,000 |
| Residence | 200,000 | 120,000 |
| Personal effects | 30,000 | 25,000 |
| Total assets | $355,000 | $245,000 |

| *Liabilities and Net Worth* | | |
|---|---|---|
| Credit cards | $1,500 | $1,000 |
| Income taxes—current year balance | 5,500 | 4,000 |
| Demand note payable to bank, 16% | 10,000 | — |
| Mortgage payable, 10% (Note 2) | 100,000 | 110,000 |
| Total | 117,000 | 115,000 |
| Estimated income taxes on the differences between the estimated current values of assets, the current amounts of liabilities, and their tax bases (Note 3) | 10,000 | 5,000 |
| Net worth | 228,000 | 125,000 |
| Total liabilities and net worth | $355,000 | $245,000 |

The notes to financial statements are an integral part of these statements.

Source: The illustrative statements are taken from Statement of Position 92-1: Accounting and Financial Reporting for Personal Financial Statements (New York: AICPA, 1982), Appendix A. Copyright © 1982 by the American Institute of Certified Public Accountants, Inc., reprinted with permission.

should identify the entity as a development stage enterprise and describe the nature of development stage activities. During the first period of normal operations, the enterprise must disclose in notes to the financial statements that the enterprise was but is no longer in the development stage. Exhibit 11.2 illustrates a balance sheet for a development stage company.

---

**Exhibit 11.2**

---

**Income Statement for a Development Stage Company**

**ALLEN COMPANY**
**(A Development Stage Company)**
**Income Statement**

| | Year Ended December 31 | | Total from Inception (October 1, 19X1 to |
| | --- | --- | --- |
| | 19X4 | 19X3 | December 31, 19X4) |
| **Revenues:** | | | |
| Sales | $150,000 | $ — | $150,000 |
| Interest | 50,000 | 60,000 | 210,000 |
| Total revenues | 200,000 | 60,000 | 360,000 |
| | | | |
| **Expenses:** | | | |
| Initial manufacturing | 80,000 | 50,000 | 130,000 |
| Marketing | 100,000 | 90,000 | 300,000 |
| General and Administrative (including preoperating) | 300,000 | 300,000 | 1,000,000 |
| Total expenses | 480,000 | 440,000 | 1,430,000 |
| Net loss during development stage | $280,000 | $380,000 | $1,070,000 |
| Weighted average number of shares outstanding | 100,000 | 95,000 | |
| Net loss per share | $2.80 | $4.00 | |

---

## COMPANIES IN FINANCIAL DISTRESS

An increasing number of corporations, municipalities, colleges, and other institutions are experiencing financial distress. While there are undoubtedly as many causes of financial distress as there are enterprises experiencing distress, the following factors have been identified as usually directly or indirectly involved.

1. Financing problems—difficulties in meeting obligations:
   a. Liquidity deficiency
   b. Equity deficiency
   c. Debt default
   d. Funds shortage

2. Operating problems—apparent lack of operating success:
   a. Continued operating losses
   b. Prospective revenues doubtful
   c. Ability to operate is jeopardized
   d. Incapable management
   e. Poor control over operations

Specific signs of financial distress in an enterprise include the following: liquidation process began, a declining share of major product markets, deferment of payments to short-term creditors, omission of preferred dividends, the filing of Chapter 7 or Chapter 11 bankruptcy, efforts to dispose of a segment of a business, bond default, overdrawn bank account, insolvency, and illiquidity. The financially healthy firm usually has an adequate return on investment and a sound balance sheet.

An examination of the financial statements along with evidence obtained from management and other sources can provide the analysts with a basis for evaluating the going-concern condition of an enterprise. As a general rule, the assumption that an entity is a going concern is made in the absence of evidence to the contrary. Research in business failures indicates that cash flow to total debt ratios, capital structure ratios, and liquidity ratios are good predictors of bankruptcy and bond default. Turnover ratios are not particularly helpful in predicting financial distress. Bond rating changes and bond ratings of new issues can frequently be predicted by the use of ratios. In the final analysis, cash flows and the ability to obtain cash are the critical events associated with a distressed company's financial viability.

In certain industries, regulatory bodies have been established to monitor financial solvency and stability of companies. State insurance commissioners are usually authorized to evaluate registered insurance companies in a particular state. The Interstate Commerce Commission evaluates railroads' ability to remain viable economic units. The Federal Deposit Insurance Corporation is deeply involved with the evaluation of banks coming under its jurisdiction. Various state agencies also have regulatory authority over state banks.

The analyst involved with companies in bankruptcy or close to bankruptcy must understand the bankruptcy process. Bankruptcy is a judicial procedure used to reconcile the conflicting interests that occur when a debtor has incurred too much debt. The Bankruptcy Reform Act of 1978 is the major federal law dealing with bankruptcy. The public policy goal of bankruptcy is to give the debtor a "fresh start" in financial dealings and to obtain a fair distribution of the debtor's assets among the creditors. A discharge in bankruptcy refers to the absolution of a bankrupt's debt, by court order, upon the liquidation or rehabilitation of the bankrupt.

A **bankrupt** is a person recognized by law as being unable to pay debts. A business is insolvent in the legal sense when the financial condition is such that the sum of the entity's debts is greater than the entity's property at fair valuation. All federal bankruptcy cases must be filed under a specific chapter of the Reform Act. In Chapter 7 of the Reform Act, the assets of the debtor are liquidated in an effort to satisfy creditors. Chapter 11 provides for the reorganization of the debtor's finances and operations so that it can continue operating. Chapter 13 provides for the adjustment of debts of an individual with regular income to enable the person to work through financial problems while avoiding liquidation. Chapter 9 applies to municipalities and sets forth the procedures for the rehabilitation of a financially troubled municipality.

The Reform Act established a new bankruptcy court system. Special bankruptcy courts are located in each federal judicial district. These courts have judicial authority over all cases and proceedings brought under the Act. The courts have exclusive authority over all property of the debtor.

Chapter 7 liquidation cases begin voluntarily when a debtor corporation files a petition with the bankruptcy court or involuntarily when three or more entities file the petition. In Chapter 7 cases, the estate of the debtor corporation is turned over to an interim trustee until a trustee is elected by unsecured creditors. A Chapter 11 reorganization case can be initiated either voluntarily by a debtor or involuntarily by creditors. In Chapter 11 cases, a trustee may be appointed for cause; otherwise, the debtor corporation continues in possession.

A **statement of affairs** is a report prepared to show the immediate liquidation amounts of assets, instead of historical costs, and the estimated amounts that would be received by each class of claim or party of interest in the event of the liquidation of an enterprise. The report is essentially a

balance sheet prepared on the assumption that the enterprise is to be liquidated rather than on the going-concern assumption normally applied to the
preparation of financial statements. Emphasis is placed on the legal status of
resources and claims against those resources. Creditors and owners can use
the statement to estimate the amounts that could be realized on the disposi-
tion of the assets and the priority of claims as well as any estimated deficiency that would result if the enterprise were to be liquidated. A typical
statement of affairs discloses the following information about assets and
liabilities:

**Assets**
Assets pledged with fully secured creditors
Assets pledged with partially secured creditors
Free assets

**Liabilities**
Liabilities having priorities
Fully secured liabilities
Partially secured creditors
Unsecured creditors

A trustee or receiver is usually required to prepare a **realization and liquidation account** or report to summarize his or her activities during a reporting period. The report typically discloses the following information:

### Realization and Liquidation Account

| | |
|---|---|
| Assets to be realized | Assets realized |
| Assets acquired | Assets not realized |
| Liabilities liquidated | Liabilities to be liquidated |
| Liabilities not liquidated | Liabilities incurred |
| Supplementary charges (expenses) | Supplementary credits (revenues) |

## *BUSINESS COMBINATIONS*

A **business combination** occurs when a corporation and one or more incor-
porated or unincorporated businesses are brought together into one accounting entity. The single entity carries on the activities of the previously
separate, independent enterprises. Business combinations can be classified
structurally into three types: horizontal, vertical, and conglomerate. A **horizontal combination** is one that involves companies within the same indus-

try that have previously been competitors; a **vertical combination** involves a company and its suppliers or customers; a combination resulting in a **conglomerate** is one involving companies in unrelated industries having few, if any, production or market similarities.

**MERGERS, CONSOLIDATIONS, AND ACQUISITIONS.** Business combinations can be classified by method of combination as statutory mergers, statutory consolidations, and stock acquisitions. A statutory **merger** occurs when one company acquires all the net assets of one or more other companies. The acquiring company survives; the acquired company or companies cease to exist as separate legal entities. For example, a merger occurs between constituent corporations A and B if A remains the same legal entity (essentially with the combined assets and liabilities of A and B) and B goes out of existence.

A statutory **consolidation** requires the formation of a new corporation that acquires two or more corporations; the acquired corporations then cease to exist as separate legal entities. For example, Corporations A and B agree to transfer their assets and liabilities to a new corporation C and then go out of existence, leaving C as the corporation to carry on the activities of A and B.

A **stock acquisition** occurs when one corporation pays cash or issues stock or debt for more than 50 percent of the voting stock of another company and the acquired company remains intact as a separate legal entity. The relationship of the acquiring company to the acquired company in a stock acquisition is described as a **parent-subsidiary relationship**. The acquiring company is referred to as the parent (investor) and the acquired company as a subsidiary. The related companies are called affiliated companies. Each of the affiliated companies continues as a separate legal entity. The parent company carries its interest in a subsidiary as an investment in its accounts.

Consolidated financial statements are prepared only when the business combination was carried out as a stock acquisition.

The parent-subsidiary relationship can be visualized as shown in Exhibit 11.3. In the illustration, the parent company owns 90 percent of the subsidiary. A 10 percent interest in the subsidiary is owned by someone other than the parent. This interest is referred to as a **minority interest.**

The relationship between mergers, consolidations, and stock acquisitions can be summarized as follows:

## Exhibit 11.3

### Parent-Subsidiary Relationship

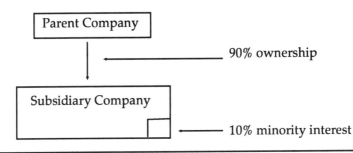

| | Prior to Combination | Survivors |
|---|---|---|
| Merger | A and B | A or B |
| Statutory consolidation | A and B | C |
| Acquisition | A and B | A and B |

**POOLING OF INTERESTS AND PURCHASE METHODS.** Two methods of accounting are available for recording a business combination—purchase and pooling of interests. The concept behind the pooling-of-interests method is that the holders of the common stock in the combining companies continue as holders of the common stock in the combined company. The business combination is accounted for by adding together the book values of the assets and equities of the combined enterprises. The combining corporation records the assets and liabilities received from the combined companies at book values recorded on the books of the combined company. The equity of the acquired company is combined with the equity of the acquiring company. The allocation of the acquired company's equity among common stock, other contributed capital, and retained earnings may have to be restructured as a result of the differences in the par value of the stock issued and the par value of the stock acquired. The combining companies' prior financial statements are combined as if the companies had always been one company.

To illustrate pooling accounting, assume the following situation, in which Company A and Company B enter into a statutory consolidation and form Company C. The following data is available about Companies A and B:

| | Stockholders' Equity | | |
| | Company A | Company B | Total |
|---|---|---|---|
| Common stock | $1,000,000 | $2,000,000 | $3,000,000 |
| Other paid-in capital | 1,000,000 | 1,000,000 | 2,000,000 |
| Retained earnings | 2,000,000 | 2,000,000 | 4,000,000 |
| Total | $4,000,000 | $5,000,000 | $9,000,000 |

In this case, C acquires the net assets (assets and liabilities) of A and B in exchange for new stock having a par value of $2,000,000. C makes the following entry on its accounting records to record the business combination as a pooling of interests:

| | | |
|---|---|---|
| Net assets (listed) | 9,000,000 | |
| Common stock—Company C | | 2,000,000 |
| Other paid-in capital | | 3,000,000 |
| Retained earnings | | 4,000,000 |

Note that C records the assets at the amounts reported on A and B companies' books, or $9,000,000. The retained earnings of A and B are carried forward to C's records and become a part of C's retained earnings. Since the par value of C's common stock issued to acquire A and B was $2,000,000 and the par value of A and B common stock was $3,000,000, C records common stock at par of $2,000,000 and records $3,000,000 in other paid-in capital. The acquired companies' earnings are included with the acquiring company's earnings for the full year in which the combination occurs, regardless of when the combination occurred during the year.

Because most companies present financial summaries for a number of years (comparative financial statements), these summaries are also adjusted to reflect the combined totals of the separate combining companies as if only one company had existed in all the earlier years.

The pooling-of-interests method can be contrasted with the purchase method of accounting for a business combination, which is used under certain circumstances in accounting for a business combination. Accounting for a business combination by the purchase method follows principles normally applicable under the historical-cost method for acquisitions of assets and issuances of stock. The cost to the purchasing entity of acquiring another company in a business combination treated as a purchase is the amount of cash disbursed or the fair value of other assets distributed or securities issued. The cost of the assets recorded on the acquired companies' books is not recorded by the acquiring company as the cost of the purchased assets, as would be the case when the pooling-of-interests method is used. Since the assets acquired are recorded at their fair market value, any excess of cost over these fair values of total identifiable net assets is assigned to intangibles, such as goodwill. Goodwill is amortized over a period of years not to exceed 40. The purchase method of accounting must be used for a business combination unless all conditions prescribed for a pooling of interests are met.

In purchase accounting, post acquisition earnings of the acquired entity are combined with the surviving entity's earnings. Restatement of the financial statements of prior years is not required.

The accounting method employed in recording a business combination has many implications for the analysts. For example, under pooling accounting, assets are carried at "book value," not at current fair values that presumably reflect the consideration given in exchange for them. If fair value exceeds book value, then the acquired assets are understated and this understatement leads to an understatement of capital employed by the company and an overstatement of the return on investment. The understatement of assets such as inventory, plant, and equipment can result in an understatement of expenses, including cost of goods sold, depreciation, and amortization of goodwill, thus resulting in an overstatement of income.

The acquisition terms associated with a business combination, including debt payments or stock distributions, can greatly influence future cash flows, future income flows, growth prospects, financial stability, and other significant prospects. An understanding of the terms as well as of the accounting principles and practices associated with business combinations is essential for analysts who become involved in such situations.

## FOREIGN TRANSACTIONS AND OPERATIONS

Many U.S. companies do business with foreign firms and engage in operations outside the United States. When business transactions are undertaken abroad, accounting for these transactions by a U.S. company is done in U.S. dollars—the unit of measurement in the United States. Business transactions and foreign operations (e.g., subsidiaries and branches) that are recorded in a foreign currency must be restated in U.S. dollars in accordance with generally accepted accounting principles.

**TRANSACTIONS AND OPERATIONS.** The accountant normally becomes involved in foreign operations in one of two ways:

1.  Foreign currency transactions—A foreign currency transaction is one that requires settlement in a foreign currency. Foreign currency transactions include buying and selling, borrowing or lending, investing in a foreign enterprise in which foreign currencies are received or paid, and forward exchange contracts. Transactions are normally measured and recorded in the currency of the reporting entity. A transaction is **denominated** in a currency if the amount is fixed in terms of that currency. For example, if a transaction is to be settled by the payment of foreign currency, the U.S. firm measures and records the transaction in dollars, but the transaction is said to be denominated in the foreign currency.

2.  Translation of financial statements denominated in a foreign currency—**Translation** is the process of expressing functional currency measurements in the reporting currency for the purpose of consolidation, combination, or reporting on the equity method (one-line consolidation). The reporting currency is the currency in which an enterprise prepares its financial statements. **Functional currency** is the currency of the primary economic environment in which an entity operates. Normally, the functional currency is the currency of the environment in which an entity generates and expends cash. Translation usually becomes necessary when a U.S. company owns a branch, division, or subsidiary in a foreign country. The unit keeps its accounting records and financial statements in the foreign country's currency. The statements must be translated before the U.S. company can include the foreign operations in combined or consolidated statements.

**Foreign currency transactions** are accounted for as follows:

1.  Receivables, payable, revenues, and expenses are translated and recorded in dollars at the spot rate existing on the transaction date. An exchange rate that indicates the price of foreign currencies on a particular date for immediate delivery is called a **spot rate.**

2.  At the balance-sheet date, receivables and payables are adjusted to the spot rate.

3.  Exchange gains and losses resulting from changes in the **spot rate** from one time to another are usually recognized in the current income statement. Such gains and losses represent economic gains and losses and not merely accounting gains and losses.

**FORWARD EXCHANGE CONTRACTS.** A forward exchange contract is an agreement to exchange currencies at a specified future date and at a specified forward rate. A forward margin is the difference between to-day's price of a currency (the spot rate) and the price at some date in the future (the forward rate). The margin may be either a premium or a discount.

The accounting required for **forward exchange contracts** depends on management's intent when entering into the transaction. The recognition of exchange gains and losses on forward contracts depends on the classification of the forward contract: hedge of a net asset or liability position, hedge of an identifiable commitment (for example, the purchase or sale of equipment), hedge of a net investment in a foreign entity, and speculation. A **hedge** is an arrangement entered into to try to avoid or lessen a loss by making a counterbalancing investment or commitment. In **hedging contracts,** gain or loss is the difference between the balance-sheet date spot exchange rate and the spot exchange rate at the inception of the contract, multiplied by the amount of foreign currency involved in the transaction. In **speculative contracts,** gain or loss is the difference between the agreed-upon forward exchange rate and the forward exchange rate relating to the remaining maturity of the contract, multiplied by the amount of foreign currency involved in the transaction.

*FASB Statement No. 52,* "Foreign Currency Translation," requires that gains and losses on foreign currency **transactions** be generally included in determining net income for the period in which exchange rates change unless the transaction hedges a foreign currency commitment or a net investment in a foreign entity. A **premium or discount** on an **identifiable hedge or on the hedge of a net investment in a foreign country** is either amortized to net income over the life of the contract or recognized as part of the total gain or loss on the identifiable transaction. A premium or discount on **all other hedges** is amortized to net income over the life of the forward exchange contract.

## FOREIGN SUBSIDIARIES AND INVESTMENTS. Accounting principles for purposes of consolidation, combination, or reporting on the equity method for foreign operations can be summarized in broad terms as follows:

1.  Foreign currency financial statements must be in conformity with generally accepted accounting principles before they are translated.

2.  The functional currency of an entity is the currency of the primary economic environment in which the foreign entity operates. The functional currency may be the currency of the country in which the foreign entity is located (the local currency), the U.S. dollar, or the currency of another foreign country.

(a) If the foreign entity's operations are self-contained and integrated in a particular country and are not dependent on the economic environment of the parent company, the functional currency is the foreign currency. This type of foreign operation typically generates and spends foreign currency; the net cash flow can be reinvested, converted, or distributed to the parent company. For example, if a London subsidiary of a U.S. company purchases merchandise from a London supplier on credit, the payable will be settled with pounds sterling generated by the self-contained London subsidiary. Changes in the foreign exchange rate between dollars and pounds will have little economic significance, since dollars were not used to retire the debt.

(b) On the other hand, the functional currency of a foreign company would be the U.S. dollar if the foreign operation is an integral component or extension of the parent company's operation. The daily operations and cash flows of the foreign operation of the foreign entity are dependent on the economic environment of the parent company.

3.  The functional currency statements of the foreign entity are translated into the functional currency of the reporting entity (the U.S. company) using the **current rate of exchange method.** No actual conversion of assets or liabilities from one currency to another occurs. The current rate method requires that the current rate of exchange be used to translate the assets and liabilities of a foreign entity from its functional currency into the reporting currency. The weighted-average exchange rate for the period is used to translate revenue and expenses. Gain or loss resulting from the translation of foreign currency financial statements is not recognized in current net income. **Such gains or losses are considered accounting and not economic gains or losses.** These gains or losses are reported as a separate component of stockholders' equity.

4.  If a foreign entity's records are not kept in the functional currency, they must be **remeasured** into the functional currency prior to translation, using what is referred to as the temporal method of translation. Remeasurement is the process of measuring in the functional currency those financial statement amounts that are denominated in another currency. The **temporal method** requires that account balances be translated in a manner that retains their measurement basis. Under the temporal method, monetary assets and liabilities (such as cash, receivables, and most liabilities) expressed in the balance sheet of the foreign entity at current values are trans-

lated using the current exchange rate. Accounts that are carried at past exchange prices (historical cost) are translated at historical rates (rates that existed when the transaction occurred). This results in translating these amounts into dollars as of the date the transaction took place. Gains and losses resulting from the remeasurement are included in current income. **The gain or loss is considered an economic gain and not merely an accounting gain.** The temporal method is also used when the entity operates in a highly inflationary economy.

The distinction between remeasurement required when the functional currency is the U.S. dollar and translation when the functional currency is the local currency (foreign currency) can be illustrated as follows:

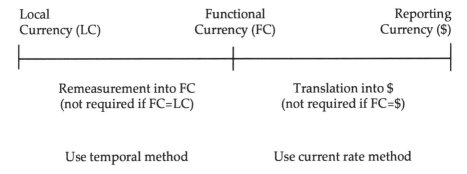

| Local Currency (LC) | Functional Currency (FC) | Reporting Currency ($) |

Remeasurement into FC
(not required if FC=LC)

Translation into $
(not required if FC=$)

Use temporal method

Use current rate method

Only when the entity's functional currency is another foreign currency (neither its local currency nor the U.S. dollar) are remeasurement and translation required (i.e., two separate numerical calculations).

**TEMPORAL METHOD ILLUSTRATED.** Exhibit 11.4 illustrates the temporal method, which assumes that **the functional currency of a Canadian subsidiary is the U.S. dollar.** The subsidiary was established at the beginning of the year. The current rate of exchange is $.80; the historical rate used for the building and common stock is $.90; the average rate for the year is $.85. The computation of the exchange loss for the year, the first year of operations, is also shown and results from the impact of rate changes on the net monetary position (monetary assets minus monetary liabilities) during the year. The $10,406 exchange loss occurred because the subsidiary held net monetary assets denominated in Canadian dollars when the Canadian dollar decreased in value relative to the U.S. dollar.

The analysts should understand that when the temporal method is used, exposure to translation gains and losses is measured by the excess of mone-

## Exhibit 11.4

### Temporal Method
### Remeasurement under FASB
### Statement No. 52

| | Canadian Dollars | Exchange Rate | U.S. Dollars |
|---|---|---|---|
| **Balance Sheet:** | | | |
| *Assets* | | | |
| Cash | C$ 77,555 | .80 | US$ 62,044 |
| Rent Receivable | 25,000 | .80 | 20,000 |
| Building (net) | 475,000 | .90 | 427,500 |
| | C$ 577,555 | | US$ 509,544 |
| | | | |
| *Liabilities and Equity* | | | |
| Accounts Payable | 6,000 | .80 | 4,800 |
| Salaries Payable | 4,000 | .80 | 3,200 |
| Common Stock | 555,555 | .90 | 500,000 |
| Retained Earnings | 12,000 | See below | 1,544 |
| | C$ 577,555 | | US$ 509,544 |
| | | | |
| **Income Statement:** | | | |
| Rent Revenue | C$ 125,000 | .85 | US$ 106,250 |
| Operating Expenses | (28,000) | .85 | (23,800) |
| Depreciation Expense | (25,000) | .90 | (22,500) |
| Translation Exchange Loss | — | See Exhibit 8.4 | (10,406) |
| Net Income | C$ 72,000 | | US$ 49,544 |
| | | | |
| **Retained Earnings Statement:** | | | |
| Balance, January 1, Year 1 | C$ — | | US$ — |
| Net Income | 72,000 | See above | 49,544 |
| Dividends | (60,000) | .80 | (48,000) |
| Balance, December 31, Year 1 | C$ 12,000 | | US$ 1,544 |

## Computation of Translation Exchange Loss for Year 1

|  | Canadian Dollars | Exchange Rate | U.S. Dollars |
|---|---|---|---|
| Net Monetary Position | | | |
| January 1, Year 1 | C$ — | | US$ — |
| Plus: | | | |
| Cash Invested by P | 555,555 | .90 | 500,000 |
| Cash and Receivable | | | |
| from Rents | 125,000 | .85 | 106,250 |
| Less: | | | |
| Cash Disbursed for Building | (500,000) | .90 | (450,000) |
| Cash Disbursed and | | | |
| Liabilities Incurred for | | | |
| Operating Expenses | (28,000) | 85 | (23,800) |
| Cash Disbursed | | | |
| for Dividends | (60,000) | .80 | (48,000) |
| Subtotal | | | 84,450 |
| Net Monetary Position, | | | |
| December 31, Year 1 | C$ 92,555 | .80 | 74,044 |
| Translation Exchange Loss | | | US$ 10,406 |

Source: Belcher, Finley E., and Stickney, Clyde P., *Business Combinations and Consolidated Financial Statements* (Richard D. Irwin, Homewood, Ill.).

---

tary assets over monetary liabilities. For example, if a foreign subsidiary has an excess of monetary assets over monetary liabilities, when:

| As against local currency | Translation effect on income statement |
|---|---|
| Dollar strengthens | Loss |
| Dollar weakens | Gain |

On a consolidated balance sheet, monetary assets and monetary liabilities are reported at the amount obtained by using the current rate of exchange. Nonmonetary assets and nonmonetary liabilities are usually reported using an exchange rate that was in existence when the transaction creating the nonmonetary item occurred. This procedure is also used when excessive inflation would cause the translation of nonmonetary assets at the current rate to result in unrealistically low values.

**CURRENT RATE METHOD ILLUSTRATED.** Exhibit 11.5 reworks the problem and assumes that the foreign currency is the functional currency. For this reason, the **current rate method** of translation is used. The exhibit also shows the computation of the translation adjustment for the year which results from the impact of the rate changes on the net monetary position (total assets minus total liabilities) during the year. The translation adjustment arises because assets and liabilities are translated at the current rate while stockholders' equity accounts (net assets) are translated at the historical rate and income statement accounts at an average rate. The net assets (equity) of the investor in the foreign subsidiary are at risk to exchange rate fluctuations and not merely the net monetary assets.

Proponents of the current rate method maintain that the use of this method will reflect most clearly the economic facts since presenting all revenue and expense items at current rates reflects the actual earnings (those that can be remitted to the home country) of a foreign operation at the time. Also, stating all items at the current rate retains the operating relationships after the translation intact with those that existed before the translation; e.g., the current ratio would be the same after translation as before translation. Critics of the current rate method claim that since fixed assets are translated at the current rate and not at the rate that existed when they were acquired, the translated amounts do not represent historical (acquisition) costs and therefore are not consistent with generally accepted accounting principles, which are based to a great extent on the application of the historical cost principle.

**IMPLICATIONS FOR ANALYSTS.** Since the temporal method states monetary assets as the current rate, proponents of this method claim that this reflects the foreign currency's ability to obtain U.S. dollars. Since historical rates are used for long-term assets and liabilities, the historical cost principle is maintained for balance sheet accounts. This reflects generally accepted accounting principles; generally accepted accounting principles are not changed by the translation process. However, the use of the temporal method distorts financial statement relationships that exist before remeasurement and after remeasurement.

Analysts should understand that when the current rate method is employed, current value accounting (and not historical cost accounting) is reflected in the financial statements. Translation gains and losses bypass the income statement. The translation exposure is measured by the size of the net equity or net investment in the foreign operation, because all balance sheet items, except the net equity, are translated at the current rate. When the current rate method is used, translated reported income will vary directly with changes in exchange rates. This translation exposure differs from

## Exhibit 11.5

**Translation of Foreign Financial Statements**
**All-Current Methodology**

| | Canadian Dollars | Exchange Rate | U.S. Dollars |
|---|---|---|---|
| **Balance Sheet:** | | | |
| *Assets* | | | |
| Cash | C$ 77,555 | .80 | US$ 62,044 |
| Rent Receivable | 25,000 | .80 | 20,000 |
| Building (net) | 475,000 | .80 | 380,000 |
| | C$ 577,555 | | US$ 462,044 |
| | | | |
| *Liabilities and Equity* | | | |
| Accounts Payable | 6,000 | .80 | 4,800 |
| Salaries Payable | 4,000 | .80 | 3,200 |
| Common Stock | 555,555 | .90 | 500,000 |
| Translation Adjustment | | See below | (59,156) |
| Retained Earnings | 12,000 | | 13,200 |
| | C$ 577,555 | | US$ 462,044 |
| | | | |
| **Income Statement:** | | | |
| Rent Revenue | C$ 125,000 | .85 | US$ 106,250 |
| Operating Expenses | (28,000) | .85 | (23,800) |
| Depreciation Expense | (25,000) | .85 | (21,250) |
| Net Income | C$ 72,000 | | US$ 61,200 |
| | | | |
| **Retained Earnings Statement:** | | | |
| Balance, January 1, Year 1 | C$ — | | US$ — |
| Net Income | 72,000 | See above | 61,200 |
| Dividends | (60,000) | .80 | (48,000) |
| Balance, December 31, Year 1 | C$ 12,000 | | US$ 13,200 |

### Computation of Translation Adjustment for S for Year 1

|                                      | Canadian Dollars | Exchange Rate | U.S. Dollars |
|--------------------------------------|------------------|---------------|--------------|
| Net Asset Position January 1, Year 1 | C$ —             |               | US$ —        |
| Plus:                                |                  |               |              |
| Cash Invested by P                   | 555,555          | .90           | 500,000      |
| Net Income                           | 72,000           | .85           | 61,200       |
| Less:                                |                  |               |              |
| Dividends                            | (60,000)         | .80           | (48,000)     |
| Subtotal                             |                  |               | 513,200      |
| Net Asset Position, December 31, Year 1 | C$ 567,555    | .80           | 454,044      |
| Translation Adjustment               |                  |               | US$ 59,156   |

Source: Belcher, Finley E., and Stickney, Clyde P., *Business Combinations and Consolidated Financial Statements* (Richard D. Irwin, Homewood, Ill.)

---

that resulting from the use of the temporal method. The risk associated with changes in exchange rates is removed from the income statement.

## *RELATED-PARTY TRANSACTIONS*

Companies sometimes engage in transactions with related parties. If related-party transactions occur, the relationships between related parties can enable one of the parties to exercise influence over the other so that it is given preferential treatment. For example, a company might sell or lease equipment to an affiliated company at a lower cost or interest rate than the affiliated company would incur elsewhere. Unless disclosed, the reliability and relevance of the financial statements would be impaired. If material, such transactions must be disclosed in the financial statements. *Related parties* include affiliates of the enterprise; entities for which investments are accounted for by the equity method used by the enterprise; trusts for the benefit of employees, such as pension and profit-sharing trusts that are managed by or under the trusteeship of management; principal owners of the enterprise; its management; members of the immediate families of principal owners of the enterprise and its management; and other parties who control or can significantly influence the management or operating policies of the other.

Related-party transactions cannot be assumed to be an arm's length transaction between independent parties because the conditions necessary for a competitive, free-market environment are not likely to exist. Examples of related-party transactions include lending money to and borrowing money from each other; selling products to and purchasing products from each other; and services provided by one related party to another without charge.

The accountant typically discloses in the notes to the financial statements the following aspects of a related-party transactions:

1.  The nature of the relationship between the transacting parties.

2.  The nature and description of the transaction.

3.  The amount of the transaction and any changes in terms and effects from the preceding period.

4.  Any amounts due from or to the related parties on the balance sheet date, and the terms of settlement.

## SUBSEQUENT EVENTS

A subsequent event is an important event that occurs between the balance sheet date and the date of issuance of the annual report. A subsequent event must have a material effect on the financial statements. A subsequent event does not include the recurring economic fluctuations associated with the economy and with free enterprise, e.g., a strike or management changes. A subsequent event is considered to be important enough that without such information the statement would be misleading if the event were not disclosed. The recognition and recording of these events requires the professional judgment of an accountant or external auditor.

There are two types of subsequent events:

1.  Events that affect the financial statements at the date of the balance sheet. This information might reveal an unknown condition or provide additional information regarding estimates or judgments. These events must be reported by adjusting the financial statements to recognize the new evidence.

2.  Events that relate to conditions that did not exist on the balance sheet date but arose subsequent to that date. These events do not require an adjustment to the financial statement. However, the effect of the event on the future period may be of such importance

that it should be disclosed in the footnote or elsewhere. Conditions reported in the balance sheet cannot be extended into the future. Examples of these events include a major fire or flood loss, a litigation settlement, and the sale of a bond or stock issued after the balance sheet date.

## *FRAUDULENT FINANCIAL REPORTING*

Fraudulent financial reporting is defined as intentional or reckless reporting, whether by act or by omission, that results in materially misleading financial statements. Fraudulent financial reporting can usually be traced to the existence of conditions in either the internal environment of the firm (e.g., inadequate internal control), or to the external environment (e.g., poor industry or overall business conditions). Excessive pressure on management, such as unrealistic profit or other performance goals, can lead to fraudulent financial reporting.

The accounting profession generally is of the opinion that it is not the responsibility of the auditor to detect fraud, beyond what can be detected with the diligent application of generally accepted auditing standards. Because of the nature of irregularities, particularly those involving forgery and collusion, a properly designed and executed audit may not detect a material irregularity. The auditor is not an insurer and the report does not constitute a guarantee that material misstatements do not exist in the financial statements. The legal system generally defines the auditors' responsibility associated with the detection of fraudulent reporting by a company.

In 1977, Congress enacted the Foreign Corrupt Practices Act to deter various illegal activities including illegal foreign political contributions, bribes, kickbacks, and other violations. Specifically, the act provides that it is a criminal offense to offer a bribe to a foreign official, foreign political party, party official, or candidate for foreign political office for the purpose of obtaining, retaining, or directing business to any person.

Certain fraudulent activities have been tried under the Racketeer Influenced Corrupt Organization Act of 1970 (RICO). This act includes most patterns of criminal activities. The main features of this legislation require that the fraud must involve an organization (two or more persons) and a pattern of criminal activities (two or more crimes). U.S. attorneys must obtain permission from the Department of Justice before prosecuting a case under RICO. The maximum sentence that can be given is 20 years and a $250,000 fine on each count.

## SUMMARY

Bank loan officers and others frequently deal with personal financial statements. The underlying accounting principles used in developing corporate financial statements are modified to some extent when personal financial statements are prepared. The analysts must understand these differences and take them into consideration when evaluating personal financial statements.

Development stage companies devote substantially all their efforts to establishing a new business. Since the principal operations of the entity have not commenced and no significant revenue has been generated, analysts must exercise extreme care in conducting an evaluation of these companies' financial statements. It is essential that analysts understand the tentative nature of the enterprise and the way accountants deal with this factor in financial statements.

Companies in financial distress are sometimes difficult to identify. In certain situations, audit reports cannot be relied on to provide adequate disclosure. When companies find themselves in financial difficulties, various judicial and nonjudicial procedures are available to assist them in dealing with the problem. Bankruptcy is a judicial process that is designed to deal with extreme cases of financial distress. Analysts must understand the intricacies of bankruptcy legislation and procedures when dealing with companies involved in this process.

Analysts should be aware that there are two generally accepted methods of accounting for business combinations, purchase and pooling of interests. A pooling of interest involves an exchange of voting common shares, the combining of stockholders' equities, and the recording of the net assets of the combining companies without revaluation. Purchase accounting records the net assets acquired at their fair values at the time of combination.

Foreign operations and transactions provide complex challenges for analysts. Before the effects of foreign exchange transactions and foreign operations can be included in the financial statements of U.S. companies, they must be converted into U.S. dollars. Generally accepted accounting principles provide guidelines and requirements for remeasurement and translation. The analyst needs to obtain:

1. Information about how rate changes affect reported operating results, e.g., the effect of weakening foreign currencies on reported sales.

2. Identification of functional currencies used for foreign operations and the extent of the exchange risk involved.

3. Availability of cash flows from foreign operations.

Related-party transactions and subsequent events should be scrutinized closely by the analysts. Finally, the analyst should always be alert to the possibility that fraudulent financial reporting is present in the financial statements. The auditor's report is not absolute assurance that the statements are what they appear to be.

# Chapter 12

## *OVERVIEW PROBLEMS WITH SOLUTIONS*

A selection of problems designed to improve one's understanding of the processes relating to financial statement analysis is presented in this chapter. Solutions to the problems are provided at the end of the problems.

### *PROBLEM I —*
### *Interpreting Financial Statement Ratios*

An analyst was interested in evaluating the solvency of a business, especially its going-concern possibilities. To assist in the evaluation, he computed the following data from the company's financial statements:

|                              | Last Year | This Year |
|------------------------------|----------:|----------:|
| Current ratio                | 3.0       | 3.4       |
| Quick ratio                  | 1.5       | .3        |
| Sales to shareholders' equity| 3.1       | 2.8       |
| Net income                   | -8.2%     | +15.2     |
| Earnings per common share    | $3.10     | $3.50     |
| Book value per common share  | +9%       | +4%       |

How can the analyst use this information to provide insights into the solvency and going-concern condition of the company?

## PROBLEM II —
## Computation of Financial Statement Ratios

The Printing Company is listed on the New York Stock Exchange. The market value of its common stock was quoted at $10 per share at December 31, 19X5, and 19X4. Printing Company's financial statements are presented in Exhibit 12.1.

An investor is considering this stock as a possible investment. Before investing in the stock, the investor thought it would be helpful to compute a selection of significant ratios for 19X5 only to help her make a decision. She selected the following ratios:

1. Current ratio.

2. Quick ratio.

3. Number of days' sales in average receivables, assuming a business year of 300 days and all sales on account.

4. Inventory turnover.

5. Book value per share of common stock.

6. Earnings per share on common stock.

7. Price-earnings ratio.

8. Dividend payout ratio.

You are asked to compute these ratios.

### Exhibit 12.1

### Statements for Problem II

### Printing Company
### BALANCE SHEET

| | December 31, | |
|---|---|---|
| **Assets** | **19X5** | **19X4** |
| Current assets: | | |
| Cash | $3,500,000 | $3,600,000 |
| Marketable securities, at cost which approximates market | 13,000,000 | 11,000,000 |
| Accounts receivable, net of allowance for doubtful accounts | 105,000,000 | 95,000,000 |
| Inventories, lower of cost or market | 126,000,000 | 154,000,000 |

| | | |
|---|---|---|
| Inventories, lower of cost or market | 126,000,000 | 154,000,000 |
| Prepaid expenses | 2,500,000 | 2,400,000 |
| Total current assets | 250,000,000 | 266,000,000 |
| Property, plant, and equipment, net of accumulated depreciation | 311,000,000 | 308,000,000 |
| Investments, at equity | 2,000,000 | 3,000,000 |
| Long-term receivables | 14,000,000 | 16,000,000 |
| Goodwill and patents, net of accumulated amortization | 6,000,000 | 6,500,000 |
| Other assets | 7,000,000 | 8,500,000 |
| Total assets | $590,000,000 | $608,000,000 |

**Liabilities and Stockholders' Equity:**

| | | |
|---|---|---|
| Current liabilities: | | |
| Notes payable | $5,000,000 | $15,000,000 |
| Accounts payable | 38,000,000 | 48,000,000 |
| Accrued expenses | 24,500,000 | 27,000,000 |
| Income taxes payable | 1,000,000 | 1,000,000 |
| Payments due within one year on long-term debt | 6,500,000 | 7,000,000 |
| Total current liabilities | 75,000,000 | 98,000,000 |
| Long-term debt | 169,000,000 | 180,000,000 |
| Deferred income taxes | 74,000,000 | 67,000,000 |
| Other liabilities | 9,000,000 | 8,000,000, |
| Total liabilities | 327,000,000 | 353,000,000 |
| Stockholders' equity: | | |
| Common stock, par value $1.00 per share; authorized 20,000,000 shares; issued and outstanding 10,000,000 shares | 10,000,000 | 10,000,000 |
| 5% cumulative preferred stock, par value $100.00 per share; $100.00 liquidating value; authorized 50,000 shares; issued and outstanding 40,000 shares | 4,000,000 | 4,000,000 |
| Additional paid-in capital | 107,000,000 | 107,000,000 |
| Retained earnings | 142,000,000 | 134,000,000 |
| Total stockholders' equity | 263,000,000 | 255,000,000 |
| Total liabilities and stockholders' equity | $590,000,000 | $608,000,000 |

### Printing Company

## STATEMENT OF INCOME AND
## RETAINED EARNINGS

| | Year ended December 31, | |
| --- | --- | --- |
| | **19X5** | **19X4** |
| Net sales | $600,000,000 | $500,000,000 |
| Costs and expenses: | | |
| Cost of goods sold | 490,000,000 | 400,000,000 |
| Selling, general, and administrative expenses | 66,000,000 | 60,000,000 |
| Other net | 7,000,000 | 6,000,000 |
| Total costs and expenses | 563,000,000 | 466,000,000 |
| Income before income taxes | 37,000,000 | 34,000,000 |
| Income taxes | 16,800,000 | 15,800,000 |
| Net income | 20,200,000 | 18,200,000 |
| | | |
| Retained earnings at beginning of period | 134,000,000 | 126,000,000 |
| Dividends on common stock | 12,000,000 | 10,000,000 |
| Dividends on preferred stock | 200,000 | 200,000 |
| Retained earnings at end of period | $142,000,000 | $134,000,000 |

*(Adapted from CMA examination)*

---

## PROBLEM III — Understanding Ratios

1.  A company's current ratio is 2.2 to 1 and quick (acid-test) ratio is 1.0 to 1 at the beginning of the year. At the end of the year, the company has a current ratio of 2.5 to 1 and a quick ratio of .8 to 1. Which of the following could help explain the divergence in the ratios from the beginning to the end of the year?

    a.  An increase in inventory during the current year.

    b.  An increase in credit sales in relationship to cash sales.

    c.  An increase in the use of trade payables during the current year.

    d. An increase in the collection rate of accounts receivable.

    e. The sale of marketable securities at a price below cost.

2. Which of the following will cause a decrease in a company's accounts receivable turnover ratio?

    a. Tightening credit standards.

    b. Enforcing credit terms more aggressively.

    c. Easing enforcement of credit terms.

    d. Factoring all accounts receivable.

    e. Requiring customers to use bank credit cards and eliminating the company's own card.

3. If, just prior to a period of rising prices, a company changed its inventory measurement method from FIFO to LIFO, the effect in the next period would be to

    a. increase both the current ratio and inventory turnover.

    b. decrease both the current ratio and inventory turnover.

    c. increase the current ratio and decrease inventory turnover.

    d. decrease the current ratio and increase inventory turnover.

    e. leave the current ratio and inventory turnover unchanged.

*The following data apply to items 4–10.*
Depoole Company is a manufacturer of industrial products and employs a calendar year for financial reporting purposes. Items 4–10 present several of Depoole's transactions during 19X8. Assume that total quick assets exceeded total current liabilities both before and after each transaction described. Further assume that Depoole has positive profits in 19X8 and a credit balance throughout 19X8 in its retained earnings account.

4. Payment of a trade account payable of $64,500 would

    a. increase the current ratio but the quick ratio would not be affected.

    b. increase the quick ratio but the current ratio would not be affected.

    c. increase both the current and quick ratios.

    d. decrease both the current and quick ratios.

    e. have no effect on the current and quick ratios.

5. The purchase of raw materials for $85,000 on open account would

    a.   increase the current ratio.

    b.   decrease the current ratio.

    c.   increase net working capital.

    d.   decrease net working capital.

    e.   increase both the current ratio and net working capital.

6.    The collection of a current accounts receivable of $29,000 would

    a.   increase the current ratio.

    b.   decrease the current ratio.

    c.   increase the quick ratio.

    d.   decrease the quick ratio.

    e.   not affect the current or quick ratios.

7.    Obsolete inventory of $125,000 was written off during 19X8. This would

    a.   decrease the quick ratio.

    b.   increase the quick ratio.

    c.   increase net working capital.

    d.   decrease the current ratio.

    e.   decrease both the current and quick ratios.

8.    The issuance of new shares in a five-for-one split of common stock would

    a.   decrease the book value per share of common stock.

    b.   increase the book value per share of common stock.

    c.   increase total stockholders' equity.

    d.   decrease total stockholders' equity.

    e.   decrease both the book value per share of common stock and total stockholders' equity.

9.    The issuance of serial bonds in exchange for an office building with the first installment of the bonds due in late 19X8 would

    a.   decrease net working capital.

    b.   decrease the current ratio.

    c.   decrease the quick ratio.

    d.   decrease all of the above.

    e.   decrease none of the above.

10. The early liquidation of a long-term note with cash would

    a. affect the current ratio to a greater degree than the quick ratio.

    b. affect the quick ratio to a greater degree than the current ratio.

    c. affect the current and quick ratios to the same degree.

    d. affect the current ratio but not the quick ratio.

    e. affect the quick ratio but not the current ratio.

11. Selected year-end data for the Bangor Company are presented below:

    | Current liabilities | $600,000 |
    |---|---|
    | Acid-test ratio | 2.5 |
    | Current ratio | 3.0 |
    | Cost of sales | $500,000 |

Bangor Company's inventory turnover ratio based upon this year-end data is

    a. 1.20.

    b. 2.40.

    c. 1.67.

    d. some amount other than those given above.

    e. not determinable from the data given.

12. A firm that has substantial leased assets that need not be capitalized would tend to

    a. overstate its debt ratio.

    b. overstate its earnings per share.

    c. overstate its return on assets.

    d. overstate its debt to tangible net worth.

    e. overstate its cash flow.

13. Stock options frequently are provided to officers of companies. Stock options that are exercised would

    a. improve the debt/equity ratio.

    b. improve earnings per share.

    c. improve the ownership interest of existing stockholders.

    d. improve the total asset turnover.

    e. improve the net profit margin.

*The following data apply to items 14 and 15*

Mr. Sparks, the owner of School Supplies, Inc., is interest in keeping control over accounts receivable. He understands that accounts receivable turnover will give a good indication of how well receivables are being managed. School Supplies, Inc., does 70 percent of its business during June, July, and August. The terms of sale are 2/10, n/60.

Net sales for the year ended December 31, 19X8, and receivables balances are given below.

| | |
|---|---:|
| Net sales | $1,500,000 |
| Receivables, less allowance for doubtful accounts of $8,000 at January 1, 19X8 | 72,000 |
| Receivables, less allowance for doubtful accounts of $10,000 at December 31, 19X8 | 60,000 |

14. The average accounts receivable turnover calculated from the data above is

    a.  20.0 times.
    b.  25.0 times.
    c.  22.7 times.
    d.  18.75 times.
    e.  20.8 times.

15. The average accounts receivable turnover computed for School Supplies, Inc., in item 14 above is

    a.  representative for the entire year.
    b.  overstated.
    c.  understated.
    d.  comparable with turnover that would be experienced in June, July, and August.
    e.  absolutely correct.

*The following data apply to items 16–22.*

The 19X9 financial statements for Johanson Co. are reproduced below.

### Johanson Company
### Statement of Financial Position
### December 31
### ($000 omitted)

|  | 19X8 | 19X9 |
|---|---|---|
| **Assets** | | |
| Current assets | | |
| Cash and temporary investments | $ 380 | $ 400 |
| Accounts receivable (net) | 1,500 | 1,700 |
| Inventories | 2,120 | 2,200 |
| Total current assets | 4,000 | 4,300 |
| Long-term assets | | |
| Land | 500 | 500 |
| Building and equipment (net) | 4,000 | 4,700 |
| Total long-term assets | 4,500 | 5,200 |
| Total assets | $8,500 | $9,500 |
| **Liabilities and Equities** | | |
| Current liabilities | | |
| Accounts payable | $ 700 | $1,400 |
| Current portion long-term debt | 500 | 1,000 |
| Total current liabilities | 1,200 | 2,400 |
| Long-term debt | 4,000 | 3,000 |
| Total liabilities | 5,200 | 5,400 |
| Stockholders' equity | | |
| Common stock | 3,000 | 3,000 |
| Retained earnings | 300 | 1,100 |
| Total stockholders' equity | 3,300 | 4,100 |
| Total liabilities and equities | $8,500 | $9,500 |

## Johanson Company
## Statement of Income and Retained Earnings
## For the Year Ended December 31, 19X9
## ($000 omitted)

| | | |
|---|---:|---:|
| Net sales | | $28,800 |
| Less: Cost of goods sold | $15,120 | |
| Selling expenses | 7,180 | |
| Administrative expenses | 4,100 | |
| Interest | 400 | |
| Income taxes | 800 | 27,600 |
| Net income | | 1,200 |
| Retained earnings January 1 | | 300 |
| Subtotal | | 1,500 |
| Cash dividends declared and paid | | 400 |
| Retained earnings December 31 | | **$1,100** |

16. The acid-test ratio for 19X9 for Johanson Co. is

    a. 1.1 to 1.
    b. .9 to 1.
    c. 1.8 to 1.
    d. .2 to 1.
    e. .17 to 1.

17. The average number of days' sales outstanding in 19X9 for Johanson Co. is

    a. 18 days.
    b. 360 days.
    c. 20 days.
    d. 4.4 days.
    e. 80 days.

18. The times interest earned ratio in 19X9 for Johanson Co. is

    a. 3.0 times.
    b. 1.0 times.
    c. 72.0 times.
    d. 2.0 times.
    e. 6.0 times.

19. The asset turnover in 19X9 for Johanson Co. is

    a. 3.2 times.
    b. 1.7 times.
    c. .4 times.
    d. 1.1 times.
    e. .13 times.

20. The inventory turnover in 19X9 for Johanson Co. is

    a. 13.6 times.
    b. 12.5 times.
    c. .9 times.
    d. 7.0 times.
    e. 51.4 times.

21. The operating income margin in 19X9 for Johanson Co. is

    a. 2.7%.
    b. 91.7%.
    c. 52.5%.
    d. 95.8%.
    e. 8.3%.

22. The dividend payout ratio in 19X9 for Johanson Co. is

    a. 100%.
    b. 36%.
    c. 20%.
    d. .8%.
    e. 33.3%.

*(Adapted from CMA examination)*

## PROBLEM IV —
## Applying Accounts Receivable Ratio

The owner of a small retail firm assembled the following information:

|  | 19X1 | 19X2 |
|---|---|---|
| Sales | $1,200,000 | $1,560,000 |
| Accounts receivable | 100,000 | 120,000 |
| Turnover ratio | 12 | 14.2 |
| Days' sales outstanding | 30 | 28 |
| Credit terms 2/10; n/30 |  |  |

How would you evaluate this information?

## PROBLEM V — Applying Inventory Ratios

The following information is available for a small manufacturing company:

|  | 19X1 | 19X2 |
|---|---|---|
| Sales | $1,200,000 | $1,560,000 |
| Inventory | 200,000 | 284,000 |
| Cost of goods sold | 881,000 | 1,000,000 |
| Inventory turnover | 4.4 | 4.1 |
| Days in inventory | 83 | 89 |

Comment on this information as it relates to the level of inventory.

## PROBLEM VI — Return-on-Investment Analysis

The following data is available for the operations and financial position of a company:

| | |
|---|---:|
| Gross sales | $110,000 |
| Net sales | 80,000 |
| Net income | 10,000 |
| Total assets | 100,000 |
| Current liabilities | 20,000 |
| Long-term debt | 60,000 |

1. Compute the return on total assets for the company.

2. Assuming the company used total assets as capital employed, complete the following:

   (a) The margin of the company is____?

   (b) The capital turnover of the company is____?

   (c) Margin × Capital turnover equals____?

   (d) If sales price and volume cannot be increased and the amount of capital employed cannot be changed, how can the company increase its return on investment to 12 percent?

   (e) If expenses cannot be reduced or sales increased, how can the company increase its return on investment to 12 percent?

## PROBLEM VII — Book Value per Share

The following information is taken from the stockholders' equity section of a corporation's balance sheet. Compute the book value per share of common stock.

| | |
|---|---|
| 8% preferred stock, $10 par value, 20,000 shares outstanding, call price $23 per share, liquating value $13 per share; dividends in arrears two years; current year's dividends not paid; cumulative and nonparticipating | $100,000 |
| Common stock, $5 par value, 100,000 shares outstanding | 500,000 |
| Contributed capital in excess of par value: | |
| Preferred stock | 10,000 |
| Common stock | 100,000 |
| Retained earnings | 90,000 |
| Reserve for contingencies | 200,000 |
| Total stockholders' equity | $1,000,000 |

## PROBLEM VIII — Leverage (Trading on the Equity)

A company has $1,000,000 of net assets financed by an issue of common stock. Income before taxes is 15 percent of net assets, or $150,000. The company is considering an investment of an additional $1 million in the firm. The company has the option of issuing 5 percent bonds at par or an additional issue of common stock. Tax rate is 50 percent.

1. Compute the rate of return on net assets if the investment is financed with (a) bonds and (b) stock.

2. If business conditions become depressed and income before taxes is 3 percent of net assets, what rate of return on investment is possible if the investment is financed by (a) bonds and (b) stock.

3. Evaluate the two methods of financing.

# PROBLEM IX — True-False

If the following statements are true, circle the T; if they are false, circle the F.

1. T F  Full or adequate disclosure means that inappropriate accounting measurements can be corrected through a description of the accounting practices used and of how that practice is wrong.

2. T F  Subsequent events do not require disclosure unless the transaction or event is life threatening to the company.

3. T F  A fair presentation of financial statements is not possible unless the statements provide adequate disclosures.

4. T F  Financial statement analysis does not require paying attention to the notes to the statements and the auditor's report.

5. T F  The company with the highest current ratio is not necessarily the company with the highest liquidity.

6. T F  A summary of significant accounting policies is required to disclose the reporting company's selection of a particular accounting practice from among several acceptable alternatives.

7. T F  The auditor's report provides evidence about the reliability of the audited financial statements.

8. T F  The reporting on industry segments became necessary when companies began diversifying their activities into several different industries rather than operating entirely in a single industry.

9. T F  Disclosures are required for interim periods to assist the efforts of the user of the interim reports in assessing progress of the enterprise toward its annual goals.

10. T F  The collection of an account receivable results in an increase in a company's current ratio.

11. T F  An interim financial report is viewed as an integral part of the annual reporting period.

12. T F  Return on investment is computed as follows: sales divided by total assets.

13. T F  Accounts receivable and inventories are included in the calculation of the acid-test (quick) ratio.

14. T F  Vertical analysis of financial statements spotlights trends and establishes relationships between items appearing on the same row of comparative financial statements.

15. T F  The usefulness of conventional financial statements is impaired during inflationary periods when the statements are not adjusted for changes in the price level.

16. T F  Trading on the equity refers to trading in the capital stock of other companies.

17. T F  The current ratio is computed by dividing current liabilities by current assets.

18. T F  Net income divided by the number of shares of common stock outstanding gives the price earnings ratio.

19. T F  Financial reporting includes more than financial statements.

20. T F  Financial statements prepared according to GAAP reflect one measurement basis, i.e., historical cost.

21. T F  Information in financial statements includes estimates and judgments.

22. T F  A disclaimer of opinion means that the auditor is of the opinion that the financial statements are not presented fairly in accordance with GAAP.

23. T F  An affirmative vote of five of the seven Financial Accounting Standard Board members is required to approve a pronouncement.

24. T F  Generally accepted accounting principles apply to small, medium-size, and large firms.

25. T F  The balance sheet reflects data at a particular moment in time.

26. T F  The income statement and the cash flows statement reflect data at a particular moment in time.

27. T F  Users of financial statements usually require nonfinancial information to assist in making investment and business decisions.

28. T F  Generally accepted accounting principles have been developed mainly in the public sector.

29. T F  A detailed report that companies file annually with the Securities and Exchange Commission is a 10-K report.

30. T F  The SEC has legal authority to establish accounting standards.

31. T F  A company's external auditors have the primary responsibility for the reliability of information presented in a company's financial statements.

32. T F  Members of the FASB are required to be CPAs.

33. T F  Relevance and reliability are the two most fundamental qualities that determine the usefulness of accounting information.

34. T F  When accounting for a business, the accountant always assumes that it is a going concern.

35. T F  The consistency principle requires all companies in the same industry to use the same accounting principles.

36. T F  The materiality convention requires that significant information that would affect the decision of an informed investor be disclosed in the financial statements.

37. T F  The conservatism convention typically requires that the accountant should anticipate no gains and provide for all losses.

38. T F  Revenue reflects increases in net assets from the main activities of a company that are not related to investments by owners.

39. T F  The conservatism convention justifies the deliberate understatement of net income and net assets.

40. T F  Information would be considered relevant if it had predictive value, feedback value, and timeliness.

41. T F  Reliability is a quality of information that assures that information is reasonably free from error and bias and faithfully represents what it claims to represent.

42. T F  An expense is an outflow of assets from an entity based on activity that represents the company's main operations.

43. T F  Elements of financial statements include assets, liabilities, revenues, expenses, gains, and losses.

44. T F  The verifiability concept requires that, to the extent possible, financial statements should be based on the results of arm's length exchange transactions.

45. T F  Revenue is ordinarily recognized when the earning process is complete or virtually complete.

46. T F  The most important information about a company should generally be disclosed in the notes to the financial statements.

47. T F  The purchase of an asset for cash is reported as a financing activity in the statement of cash flows.

48. T F  The issuance of common stock for cash is reported as a financing activity in the statement of cash flows.

49. T F  The distribution of a cash dividend is reported as a financing activity in the statement of cash flows.

50. T F  Cash flows from operating activities reported on the statement of cash flows is equal to net income reported on the income statement.

---

## SOLUTIONS TO PROBLEMS

### Problem I

The current ratio increase is a favorable sign of solvency. By itself, it does not provide much information about the going-concern position of the firm. The analyst would want to know how this ratio compared with those of competitors and of the industry. An analyst would also want to know the composition of individual current assets and current liabilities to evaluate their liquidity and maturity. The reasons for the deviation from last year to this year should be investigated.

The decline noted in the quick ratio is disturbing and indicates a weakening in the liquidity of the firm. This decrease could indicate a critical decline in the cash position of the firm. A cash ratio computed by dividing cash by current liabilities would be informative. It would also be helpful to investigate what happened to inventories, since inventories are included in the current ratio and excluded from the quick ratio. It appears that there might have been a significant increase in inventory from year to year. The going-concern position of this company might be in jeopardy.

The decrease in the ratio of sales to owners' equity is unfavorable. The decline could possibly be due primarily to a decline in sales. However, since net income increased, there could be other factors at play here. This ratio provides more insight into the going-concern position of the firm than it does to the solvency of the enterprise.

The continuing increase in net income is a positive sign for both solvency and going-concern prospects. This is also a positive sign for cash flow, but the condition of accounts receivable is unknown. If sales did decline, as was mentioned earlier as a possibility, management must have reduced costs to bring about the increase. The borrowing position of the firm could be enhanced as a result of the improved operating results. In any event, the increase in income is positive for both solvency and going-concern prospects.

The percentage change in earnings per common share, which is not identical to the percentage change in net income, indicates that there has probably been a change in the number of shares of common stock outstanding. Additional financing may have been obtained through the issuance of common stock. The effect of this on solvency and going-concern prospects is difficult to evaluate without additional information.

The smaller percentage increase in book value in the current year could result primarily from the larger base existing in the preceding year. The continuing increase in book value could reflect an increase in net assets capable of creating future earnings. It is possible that this increase could also be a positive factor for future dividend distributions. The increase in book value could be considered mildly positive with regard to solvency and going-concern prospects.

Creditors would be interested in other liquidity and activity ratios, including receivables turnover, inventory turnover, the operating cycle of the business, and capital structure and profitability ratios, including debt to equity, P/E ratio, return on investment, and others.

## Problem II

1. Current (working capital) ratio:

$$\frac{\text{Total current assets}}{\text{Total current liabilities}} = \frac{\$250,000,000}{\$75,000,000} = 3.33 \text{ to } 1$$

2. Quick (acid-test) ratio:

$$\frac{\text{Total quick (acid–test) assets}}{\text{Total current liabilities}} = \frac{\$121,500,000}{\$75,000,000} = 1.62 \text{ to } 1$$

3. Number of days' sales in average receivables:

$$\frac{\text{Average accounts receivable}}{\text{Sales on account}/300 \text{ business days}} = \frac{\$100,000,000}{\$2,000,000} = 50 \text{ days}$$

4. Inventory turnover:

$$\frac{\text{Cost of goods sold}}{\text{Average inventories}} = \frac{\$490,000,000}{\$140,000,000} = 3.50 \text{ to } 1$$

5.   Book value per share of common stock:

$$\frac{\text{Total stockholders' equity less liquidating value of preferred stock}}{\text{Common shares issued and outstanding at December 31, 19X5}} = \frac{\$259,000,000}{10,000,000} = \$25.90$$

6.   Earnings per share on common stock:

$$\frac{\text{Net income less dividends on preferred stock}}{\text{Average common shares issued and outstanding during 19X5}} = \frac{\$20,000,000}{10,000,000} = \$2.00$$

7.   Price-earnings ratio on common stock:

$$\frac{\text{Market value of common stock}}{\text{Earnings per share on common stock}} = \frac{\$10.00}{\$2.00} = 5 \text{ to } 1$$

8.   Dividend-payout ratio on common stock:

$$\frac{\text{Dividends on common stock}}{\text{Net income less dividends on preferred stock}} = \frac{\$12,000,000}{\$20,000,000} = 60\%$$

## Problem III

1.   a.   An increase in inventory financed by cash or by an increase in accounts payable could account for the ratio changes.

2.   c.   The other answers will cause accounts receivable to be less, resulting in a higher ratio.

3.   d.   Current assets will decrease because LIFO inventory in periods of rising prices will be smaller than if FIFO were used. Cost of goods sold will be higher, so the inventory turnover will be smaller.

4.   c.   The denominator of both ratios decreases; the quick ratio was greater than 1. Hence, both the current and quick ratios will increase.

5.   b.   An equal increase in the numerator and denominator will decrease the current ratio when the initial ratio was greater than 1.

6.   e.   The numerator and denominator remain unchanged. In the numerator, one current assets (cash) is exchanged for another (accounts receivable).

7.   d.   Current assets are reduced, as is the numerator of the current ratio, which decreases the current ratio. Inventory is not included in the quick ratio, so this ratio is not affected by the write off.

8.   a.   The stock split increased the number of shares outstanding in the denominator. Stockholders' equity in the numerator is unchanged.

9.   d.   The bonds due within one year are classified as a current liability. Hence, items a, b, and c are not affected.

10.   b.   Cash is reduced; current liabilities are not affected. The quick ratio is affected more because cash is a larger proportion of the numerator in the quick ratio than in the current ratio.

11.   c.   The inventory ratio is

$$\frac{\text{Cost of goods sold}}{\text{Average inventory}}$$

The value of the inventory is computed as the difference in the numerator of the current and quick ratios; the numerators are multiples of the denominators:

| | | | |
|---|---|---|---|
| Current ratio | 3.0 × 600,000 | = | $1,800,000 |
| Quick ratio | 2.5 × 600,000 | = | 1,500,000 |
| Inventory | | | $300,000 |
| Inventory turnover | $\frac{\$500,000}{\$300,000}$ | = | 1.67 |

12.   c.   Assets are smaller if the losses were capitalized.

13.   a.   Common shares outstanding are increased; the denominator in the debt/equity ratio increases. EPS decreases.

14.   a.   $\dfrac{\text{Net credit sales (\$1,500,000)}}{\text{Average receivables (80,000 + 70,000) / 2}} = 20$

15. b. Averaging reduces fluctuations in receivables. Sales and receivables are low at the end of the year.

16. d. $\dfrac{2,100}{2,400} = 0.9$

17. c. $\dfrac{360 \text{ days}}{18} = 20$

18. c. $\dfrac{1,200 + 400 + 800}{400} = 6$

19. a. $\dfrac{\text{Sales } (28,800)}{\text{Total assets } (9,500)} = 3.2 \text{ approximately}$

20. a. $\dfrac{\text{Cost of goods sold } (15,120)}{\text{Average inventory } (2,160)} = 7$

21. c. $\dfrac{2,400}{28,800} = .083$

22. c. $\dfrac{400}{1,200} = .333$

## Problem IV
Both the turnover and days' sales outstanding are favorable and improving. The company may be collecting receivables faster or its credit policy may have changed so that the customers it is attracting are paying more quickly. Accounts receivable on average are paying within the discount period. In summary, it appears that sales have increased, the rate of collection has changed, the credit policy has changed, or a combination of these factors has changed.

## Problem V
The increase in inventory level could have been caused by one or a combination of the following: sales increased, a decision was made to carry more inventory to support sales, or slow-moving items are present in the inventory.

## Problem VI

1.  $10,000/$100,000 = $10\%$

2.  To solve these problems, insert the given information in the basic comprehensive return-on-investment formula and solve for the unknown factor:

$$\text{Return on investment} = \frac{\text{Net income}}{\text{Sales}} \times \frac{\text{Sales}}{\text{Capital employed}}$$

(a)  12.5%

(b)  80%

(c)  10%

(d)  Net income must be increased to $12,000. Expenses would have to be reduced by $12,000.

(e)  Capital employed must be reduced to $83,333. Perhaps inventory or accounts receivable can be reduced.

## Problem VII

First compute the value assigned to preferred stock:

| | |
|---|---:|
| Call price ($12 per share) | $ 120,000 |
| Unpaid dividends (3 years) | 24,000 |
| Total | $ 144,000 |
| Amount assigned to common stock: | |
| Total shareholders' equity | $1,000,000 |
| Less preferred shareholders' equity | 144,000 |
| Total | $ 856,000 |

Book value per common share: $856,000/100,000 shares = $8.56 per share.

## Problem VIII

| | Bonds Issued | Stock Issued |
|---|---|---|
| 1. Income before interest expense | | |
| ($2 million × 15%) | $300,000 | $300,000 |
| Less interest ($1 million × 5%) | 50,000 | |
| Taxable income | 250,000 | 300,000 |
| Less income tax | 125,000 | 150,000 |
| Net income | $125,000 | $150,000 |
| Owners' investment | $1,000,000 | $2,000,000 |
| Rate of return on investment | 12.5% | 7.5% |
| 2. Income before interest expense | | |
| ($2 million × 3%) | $ 60,000 | $60,000 |
| Less interest | 50,000 | |
| Taxable income | 10,000 | 60,000 |
| Less income tax | 5,000 | 30,000 |
| Net income | $5,000 | $30,000 |
| Owners' investment | $1,000,000 | $2,000,000 |
| Rate of return on investment | .005% | .015% |

3. The first case indicated that positive leverage existed that increased the rate of return from 7.5 percent to 12.5 percent. However, if a business recession or depression occurs, as suggested in the second case, the leverage advantage disappears and turns negative. Leverage can work both ways.

## PROBLEM IX
1. F
2. F
3. T
4. F
5. T
6. T
7. T

8. T
9. T
10. F, No effect.
11. T
12. F, Net income/total assets.
13. F, Inventories are excluded.
14. F
15. T
16. F
17. F
18. F
19. T
20. F
21. T
22. F
23. T
24. T
25. T
26. F, For a period of time.
27. T
28. F, The private sector.
29. T
30. T
31. F
32. F
33. T
34. F
35. F
36. T
37. T

38.  T

39.  F

40.  T

41.  T

42.  T

43.  T

44.  T

45.  T

46.  F, The body of the financial statements.

47.  F, An investing activity.

48.  T

49.  T

50.  F

# GLOSSARY

ACCELERATED DEPRECIATION—a depreciation method that produces progressively smaller amounts of depreciation expense each accounting period. Examples of accelerated depreciation include sum-of-the-years' digits method and the double-declining-balance method.

ACCOUNT—a form or place used to collect and record data arising from transactions affecting a single item, such as cash, inventory, accounts receivable, etc.

ACCOUNTING—an information system that measures, processes, and communicates economic information about an identifiable entity to permit users of the system to make informed judgments and decisions.

ACCOUNTING CHANGES—changes in accounting caused by changing accounting principles, estimates, or entity.

ACCOUNTING CONCEPTS—broad fundamental concepts that provide a basis for generally accepted accounting principles.

ACCOUNTING CYCLE—the sequence of events beginning with initial recognition of transactions, events, and circumstances in the accounting system and ending with the preparation of the financial statements.

ACCOUNTING ENTITY—the unit or organization that is being accounted for.

ACCOUNTING EQUATION—the underlying structure for the conventional accounting system: Assets = Liabilities + Owners' Equity.

ACCOUNTING PERIOD—the time period for which financial statements are prepared.

ACCOUNTING POLICIES—the specific accounting principles and practices adopted by a business or accounting entity.

ACCOUNTING PRINCIPLES—concepts, methods, and procedures that have become generally accepted as the basis for recording business transactions for the preparation of financial statements. *See* Generally Accepted Accounting Principles.

ACCRUAL BASIS OF ACCOUNTING—a method of recording revenues when earned and expenses when incurred. The method contrasts with the cash basis of accounting, which recognizes revenue when cash is received and expenses when cash is paid.

ACCRUED EXPENSES—expenses that are recognized prior to collection of cash.

ACCRUED REVENUE—revenue that is recognized prior to the collection of cash.

ACCUMULATED DEPRECIATION—a contra-asset account that is deducted from long-lived assets for balance-sheet presentation. The balance in the account represents the sum of the depreciation expense recorded that is related to the long-lived assets to date.

ACID-TEST RATIO—a measure of a company's immediate short-term liquidity computed by dividing the sum of cash, marketable securities, and receivables by current liabilities.

ADVERSE OPINION—an auditor's opinion that is given when the financial statements do not present fairly the results of operations, financial position, and cash flows. Material exceptions require an adverse opinion on the statements because the statements taken as a whole are not presented in accordance with GAAP.

AGING THE RECEIVABLES—the process of analyzing the accounts receivable and classifying them according to various age groupings, with the due date being the base point for determining age.

ALLOCATION—the process of assigning costs and revenues to time periods, activities, departments, etc., according to benefits received, responsibilities assumed, usage, or other ratio measures.

AMORTIZATION—the periodic expense attributed to the decline in the usefulness of an intangible asset; or of the balance of unamortized discount on bonds payable.

ANNUAL REPORT—a report prepared for stockholders and others that a company prepares annually following the end of the fiscal year. The report typically includes a letter to the shareholders from the chairman of the board, management's discussion of previous financial performance and condition, financial highlights, the basic financial statements, and the auditor's report, which expresses an opinion on the fairness of the financial statements.

ANNUITY—a stream of level payments; cash flows that are equal in each period.

ANNUITY DUE—an annuity whose first payment occurs at the end of the first period.

ANNUITY IN ARREARS—an ordinary annuity whose first payment occurs at the end of the first period.

APPROPRIATION OF RETAINED EARNINGS—restriction or reservation of an amount of retained earnings by the board of directors. The amount appropriated is not available for the declaration of dividends.

ARM'S LENGTH TRANSACTIONS—Exchanges between parties who are independent of each other and who act in their own best economic interest.

ARTICULATION OF FINANCIAL STATEMENTS—the relationship of the financial statements to each other. For example, the statement of cash flows reflects how changes throughout the balance sheet have affected cash.

ASSET—probable future economic benefit obtained or controlled by a particular entity as a result of past transactions or events.

ASSET TURNOVER RATIO—a measure of how efficiently a company uses its assets to produce sales computed by dividing net sales by average assets.

ATTEST—a written statement that indicates a conclusion about an assertion of another party, e.g., an audit opinion.

AUDIT—a comprehensive review, on a test basis, of evidence regarding the amounts and disclosures in an enterprise's financial statements for the purpose of expressing an opinion on the statements. Audits are performed by independent certified public accountants. An audit lends credibility to the company's general-purpose financial statements.

AUDIT COMMITTEE—a major committee of the board of directors of a corporation composed of outside directors who are assigned responsibilities related to the audit and auditors.

AUDITOR—a person or firm who conducts an audit to check the accuracy, fairness, and acceptability of accounting records and statements and attests to them.

AUDITOR'S REPORT—a statement made by an independent certified public accounting firm that expresses an opinion, using standardized terminology, that (1) the firm has examined the records upon which a company's financial statements were prepared, and (2) expresses an opinion on its fairness.

AUTHORIZED SHARES—the number of shares of each category of stock that a corporation can issue according to its charter.

BAD DEBT EXPENSE—an estimate of the amount of credit sales made during the accounting period or its accounts receivable that will eventually prove to be uncollectible.

BALANCE SHEET—a financial statement that provides information about an entity's assets, liabilities, and equity and their relationships to each other at a moment in time. Assets – liabilities = owners' equity.

BETA—the measure of market risk.

BOND—a promise to pay a given sum of money at some future date and to pay periodic interest amounts for the use of funds.

BOOK VALUE—total assets of a company less total liabilities, sometimes referred to as carrying value. The term is also applied to specific assets or liabilities.

BREAKEVEN ANALYSIS—financial analysis involving the computation of the amount of sales required to cover all fixed and variable costs without making a profit or loss.

BREAKEVEN POINT—a level of sales at which revenue equals expense.

BUDGET—a forecast of estimated income and expenses or financial position for a defined period of time. A comprehensive budget is a master budget or forecast that reflects a firm's plans, statements, and their components for a period. A cash budget is a forecast of expected cash receipts and disbursements for a period of time.

CALL PREMIUM ON STOCK—the difference between the par value of callable preferred stock and the amount that would be paid to the shareholders if a corporation decided to repurchase its callable preferred stock.

CAPITAL—ownership equity in a business.

CAPITAL BUDGETING—long-term planning for capital expenditures and for the financing of such expenditures.

CAPITAL LEASE—a lease that is, in substance, a sale of property from the lessor to the lessee.

CAPITAL STOCK—all of a corporation's stock including common and preferred stock.

CARRYING VALUE—the amount at which an item is valued on a company's books and reported in the financial statements.

CASH BASIS—a method of accounting that recognizes transactions only when cash is received or paid.

CASH BREAKEVEN POINT—fixed costs minus any noncash expenses divided by contribution margin or contribution margin ratio.

CASH FLOWS STATEMENT—a financial report that shows the sources and uses of cash during an accounting period.

CASH PROVIDED BY OPERATIONS—a source of financial resources disclosed on a statement of changes in financial position. The amount is computed by adding back to net income the items on the income statement that did not result in an outflow of cash and subtracting the items on the income statement that did not provide an inflow of cash.

CLASSIFIED FINANCIAL STATEMENTS—financial statements on which accounts are grouped by category within the statements.

COMMON-SIZE STATEMENTS—financial statements prepared using percentages instead of dollars.

COMMON STOCK—the basic stockholders' interest that gives shareholders voting rights and represents the residual owners' equity in a corporation.

COMPARABILITY—a quality of information that enables users to identify similarities in and differences between two sets of economic phenomena.

COMPARATIVE FINANCIAL STATEMENTS—financial statements that show data for two or more accounting periods.

COMPENSATED ABSENCES—vacations, holidays, sick days, and other absences from work during which time the regular salary or wage of the employee is continued.

COMPOUND INTEREST—interest calculated on the principal plus accumulated interest.

CONSERVATISM—the accounting principle that requires prudence or caution in financial reporting to ensure that uncertainty and risks inherent in business situations are adequately considered. It requires that the accountant select the alternative that has the least favorable impact on income or financial position.

CONSISTENCY—a basic accounting principle that requires that the financial statements be prepared in a similar manner from year to year. This requires a degree of conformity from period to period with unchanging accounting policies and procedures.

CONSOLIDATED FINANCIAL STATEMENTS—financial statements that integrate the statements of a parent and its subsidiaries.

CONSTANT-DOLLAR ACCOUNTING—an accounting procedure that adjusts historical costs to account for the general effects of inflation. It is also referred to as general-price-level accounting.

CONSTANT DOLLARS—dollars that have been adjusted for changes in the general price level. Such dollars are expressed in the same purchasing power.

CONTINGENT LIABILITIES—liabilities for which future outcomes and amounts owed are uncertain.

CONTRA-ACCOUNT—an account whose balance is deducted from the balance of another account. Accumulated depreciation, discounts on bonds payable, and the allowance for uncollectible accounts are examples of contra accounts.

CONTRIBUTED CAPITAL—that portion of stockholders' equity contributed by the owners. It is commonly referred to as *paid-in capital.*

CONTRIBUTION MARGIN—the excess of revenue over variable expenses. The contribution margin ratio is the percentage of each sales dollar available to cover fixed costs and provide an operating income; it is computed by dividing the contribution margin per unit by selling price per unit.

CONTROLLABLE COST—cost over which a manager has full control.

CONTROLLER—the chief management accountant of an entity, division, or segment of an entity.

CONVERTIBLE PREFERRED STOCK—preferred stock whose terms of issuance give the preferred stockholders the right to convert stock into a specified number of shares of common stock during a specified future period of time.

CORPORATION—an artificial legal entity separate and distinct from its owners.

COST—a sacrifice measured by the price paid or required to be paid to acquire goods or services; an exchange price related to the acquisition of assets and liabilities.

COST ACCOUNTING—an accounting process that deals with reporting, processing, and controlling the cost of a process, job, unit, or department of a firm.

COST BEHAVIOR—the manner in which costs respond to changes in activity or volume.

COST/BENEFIT—a concept that requires that the value derived from an activity must be equal to or greater than its cost.

COST CENTER—a segment or area of activity for which costs are assigned.

COST OF CAPITAL—average cost rate per year a company must pay for its equities.

COST OF GOODS SOLD—an amount calculated by subtracting the merchandise inventory at the end of the year from the goods available for sale (beginning inventory plus net purchases) during the period.

COST-VOLUME-PROFIT ANALYSIS—an analytical approach that deals with relationships among variations in revenue, expenses, and sales volume.

CUMULATIVE PREFERRED STOCK—preferred stock on which all dividends not paid in prior years must be paid along with the current year's dividends before dividends are distributed to common stockholders.

CURRENT ASSETS—cash or other assets that are expected to be realized in cash or sold during a normal operating year of a business or within one year if the operating cycle is shorter than one year.

CURRENT LIABILITIES—obligations due within the normal operating cycle of the business or within a year, whichever is longer.

CURRENT RATIO—a measure that expresses the relationship of current assets to current liabilities by dividing current assets by current liabilities.

CURRENT TAX EXPENSE—the amount of income taxes paid or payable (or refundable for a year) as determined by applying the provisions of the tax law to taxable income or excess of deductions over revenues for that year.

CURRENT VALUE ACCOUNTING—an accounting procedure that restates historical costs in terms of their current market values.

DEBT RATIOS—a ratio of long-term debt to long-term debt and equity that measures the investment of bondholders relative to the investment of stockholders; the ratio of total debt to total assets that measures the interest of all creditors, not just bondholders, in the assets of the company.

DEBT-TO-TOTAL-ASSETS RATIO—a measure of the percentage of total assets provided by creditors by dividing total debt by total assets.

DEFEASANCE—the extinguishment of debt. In-substance defeasance refers to the irrevocable placement of assets into a trust for the purpose of paying interest and principal on the debt. The debtor does not actually pay the creditor.

DEFERRED EXPENSE—an asset created through the payment of cash prior to the time at which benefits will be obtained from the expenditure. It is commonly referred to as prepaid expense.

DEFERRED REVENUE—a liability that arose through the receipt of cash prior to performance of a service or the sale of a product. It is commonly referred to as unearned revenue.

DEFERRED TAX ASSET—the amount of deferred tax consequences attributable to temporary differences that will result in net tax deductions in future years that could be recovered (based on operating loss carryback provisions in the tax law) by refund of taxes paid in the current or a prior year.

DEFERRED TAX LIABILITY—the amount of deferred tax consequences attributable to temporary differences that will result in net taxable amounts in future years. The liability is the amount of taxes that would be payable on those net taxable amounts in future years based on the provisions of the currently enacted tax law.

DEFINED BENEFIT PENSION PLAN—a pension plan that specifically states either the benefits to be received by employees after retirement or the method of determining such benefits.

DEFINED CONTRIBUTION PENSION PLAN—a pension plan wherein the employer's contribution is determined on the basis of a specified formula, and any future benefits are limited to those contributions and the returns earned on the contributions.

DEPLETION—the process of allocating the cost of a natural resource or wasting asset to inventory as the asset is reduced.

DEPRECIATION—the process of allocating the cost of a tangible fixed asset, less salvage value, over its estimated useful life in a rational and systematic manner.

DISCLAIMER OF OPINION—a statement issued by an auditor that the auditor has not been able to obtain sufficient competent evidential matter and that the auditor is unable to express an opinion. Auditors must explain the reasons for not giving an opinion.

DISCONTINUED OPERATIONS—the discontinuance of a major portion of an entity's operations. The results of discontinued operations should be separated from the operating results of continuing operations. Any gain or loss on the disposal of the discontinued part of the business should also be shown separately.

DISCOUNTED CASH FLOW METHOD—an approach to capital budgeting that discounts expected future cash flows to their present values.

DIVIDEND—a distribution of assets from retained earnings to shareholders. A stock dividend does not involve the distribution of assets but merely involves the issuance of additional shares of a company's own stock.

DIVIDENDS IN ARREARS—dividends on cumulative preferred stock that have not been paid in prior years.

DOUBLE-ENTRY ACCOUNTING—a system of accounting that requires the financial impact of every transaction to be recorded in the accounts by equal amounts placed on the left side of some account(s) and the right side of (an)other account(s).

EARNING RATIOS—ratios that measure the return on assets, stockholders' equity, investment, and other accounting and financial categories.

EARNINGS PER SHARE—that portion of a corporation's net income that relates to each share of common stock outstanding.

EFFECTIVE INTEREST RATE—the actual rate of interest earned taking into consideration premiums or discounts on the debt. The effective rate may be higher or lower than the stated interest rate on the face of the security. This rate is sometimes referred to as the **market rate.**

EFFICIENCY—optimal relationship between inputs and outputs.

ELEMENT OF FINANCIAL STATEMENTS—the building blocks with which financial statements are constructed—the classes of items that financial statements present: assets, liabilities, equity, revenues, gains, expenses, losses, investments by owners, distribution to owners, and comprehensive income.

ENTITY—the focus of the accounting process, e.g., a corporation, partnership, or sole proprietorship.

EQUITY—the residual interest in the assets of an entity that remains after deducting its liabilities. In a business enterprise, the equity is the ownership interest.

EQUITY METHOD—an accounting method for long-term investments in stock according to which a proportionate share of the earnings of the investee is included in the investor's income. Dividends from the investee are not considered income but are treated as a reduction of the investment account.

EQUITY RATIOS—ratios that provide measures of return on stockholders' investment, earnings per share, book value per share, price-earnings ratio, and others related to stockholders' equity.

ERRORS—unintentional misstatements or omissions in financial statements, such as oversights, misinterpretation of facts, and mistakes in the application of accounting principles.

ETHICS—a discipline dealing with moral duty, right, and wrong.

EXPENSE—outflows or other using up of assets or incurrences of liabilities (or a combination of both) during a period from delivering or producing goods, rendering services, or carrying out other activities that constitute the entity's ongoing major or central operations.

EXTERNAL REPORTING—financial reporting to stockholders and other parties outside an enterprise.

EXTRAORDINARY ITEMS—material items that are both unusual in nature and infrequent in occurrence, taking into consideration the economic environment of the company.

FICA TAX—the Federal Insurance Contributions Act tax used to finance federal programs for old age and disability benefits—social security and health insurance for the aged (Medicare).

FINANCIAL ACCOUNTING—a branch of accounting that provides external users with qualitative information regarding an enterprise's economic resources, obligations, and financial performance.

FINANCIAL ACCOUNTING STANDARDS BOARD (FASB)—a seven-member organization that was established by the accounting profession to establish accounting principles that represent generally accepted reporting practices.

FINANCIAL ASSET—an intangible asset the future benefit of which is a claim to future cash. Financial assets include debt and equity claims.

FINANCIAL FLEXIBILITY—the capacity to adapt to favorable and unfavorable changes in operating conditions.

FINANCIAL STATEMENT ANALYSIS—a term used to describe techniques that disclose significant relationships in financial statements and permit comparisons from period to period and among companies.

FINANCIAL STATEMENTS—reports by which companies communicate information to users, especially investors and creditors.

FINANCIAL STRUCTURE—the liabilities and equity of an enterprise that reflect the way in which assets are being financed.

FINANCING ACTIVITIES—cash flow activities that are associated with liability and stockholders' equity items and include obtaining cash from creditors and repaying amounts borrowed and obtaining capital from owners and proving them with a return on their investment.

FIRST-IN, FIRST-OUT (FIFO)—an inventory costing method by which the cost of ending inventory is determined from the cost of the most recent purchase, and cost of goods sold is determined from the cost associated with the oldest purchases, including beginning inventory.

FOOTNOTES—notes or informative disclosures appended to and considered a part of financial statements. Footnotes typically provide information concerning such matters as depreciation and inventory methods used, details of long-term debt, pensions, leases, income taxes, contingent liabilities, method of consolidation, and other matters.

FORECAST—an estimate. *See* Budget.

FORWARD EXCHANGE CONTRACT (FUTURE)—a contract involving the purchase or sale of foreign currency for future delivery. The forward rate is the price quoted currently for future purchase or sale of a foreign currency.

FULL DISCLOSURE—an accounting principle that requires that adequate disclosure be made of anything that would be of interest to an informed investor.

FUNCTIONAL CURRENCY—the currency in use in the primary economic environment of a foreign operation.

FUTURE VALUE—the amount that an investment will be worth at a future date if invested at compound interest.

GAIN—increases in equity (net assets) from peripheral or incidental transactions of an entity and from all other transactions and other events and circumstances affecting the entity during a period except those that result from revenues or investments by owners.

GENERAL PRICE INDEX—a measure of aggregate prices of a wide range of goods and services at one time relative to prices during a base period.

GENERAL PRICE-LEVEL CHANGES—changes in the aggregate prices of a wide range of goods and services in the economy.

GENERAL PURCHASING POWER OF THE DOLLAR—the purchasing power of a dollar over a wide range of goods and services in the economy. The general purchasing power of the dollar is inversely related to the change in a general price index.

GENERAL PURPOSE FINANCIAL STATEMENT—financial statements prepared primarily for general users of the financial statements of a company, usually considered to be investors and creditors.

GENERALLY ACCEPTED ACCOUNTING PRINCIPLES (GAAP)—the conventions, rules, and procedures that reflect a consensus at a particular time about the correct way to report information on financial statements. Responsibility for the development of authoritative generally accepted accounting principles is primarily the responsibility of the Financial Accounting Standards Board.

GOING-CONCERN ASSUMPTION—the accounting assumption that the entity will continue to operate in the future.

GOODWILL—an intangible asset representing the excess of the cost of acquiring a business over the fair market value of the identifiable net assets acquired.

GROSS MARGIN—the excess of sales revenue over cost of goods sold. Gross margin analysis establishes the relationship between sales, cost of goods sold, and gross margin.

HEDGING—the process of protecting transactions or assets against future fluctuations in the market.

HISTORICAL COST—an accounting principle that measures the value of an item by reference to its original purchase or acquisition price.

HOLDING GAIN (LOSS)—the increase (decrease) in the value of an asset from the time of its acquisition or prior measurement to the date of its sale or current measurement.

HORIZONTAL ANALYSIS—a method for evaluating a series of financial statement data over a period of time to determine the amount and/or percentage increase (decrease) that has occurred.

INCOME STATEMENT—a financial statement that shows revenues, expenses, and net income (loss) for a business over an accounting period.

INCOME-TAX EXPENSE (OR BENEFIT)—the sum of income taxes payable (or refundable) and deferred tax expense (or benefit).

INCOME TAXES PAYABLE (OR REFUNDABLE)—the amount of income tax paid or payable (or refundable) for a year as determined by applying the provisions of the tax law to the taxable income or operating loss for that year. Sometimes called current tax expense (or benefit).

INFLATION—a period of gradually rising prices.

INFORMATION SYSTEM—a system for collecting, processing, and communicating data.

INTANGIBLE ASSET—a long-term, nonphysical asset used in the operations of a business and that is not for sale. Examples of intangible assets include patents, copyrights, goodwill, and trademarks.

INTERIM FINANCIAL STATEMENTS—financial statements for periods of less than a year, usually quarterly.

INTERNAL CONTROL—the detailed policies and procedures used by an enterprise to direct operations and provide reasonable assurance that the enterprise's objectives are achieved. The internal control structure of an enterprise consists of the accounting system, the control environment, and the control procedures.

INTERNAL RATE OF RETURN—the discount rate that equates the net present value of cash inflows and outflows to zero.

INTERPERIOD TAX ALLOCATION—the allocation of income tax expense among periods to compensate for a temporary difference between reported book income and taxable income.

INVENTORY TURNOVER—a measure of the liquidity of inventory by dividing cost of goods sold by average inventory.

INVESTING ACTIVITIES—cash flows that include lending and collecting loans and acquiring and disposing investments and productive long-lived assets.

JOURNAL—a book of original entry in which transactions and events are first recorded.

LAST-IN, FIRST-OUT (LIFO)—an inventory costing method by which the cost of the ending inventory is determined from the cost of the oldest purchases, including beginning inventory, and the cost of goods sold is determined from the cost of the most recent purchases.

LEDGER—the book containing a company's accounts.

LEVERAGE—an activity that borrows funds at a specified interest rate with the expectation of using these funds to earn a higher rate of return for the benefit of the enterprise. The term also applies to an activity that obtains funds through the issuance of preferred stock at a specified dividend rate with the expectation of earning a higher rate of return through the use of such funds for the benefit of common stockholders. Financial leverage is the ratio of debt to equity; the ratio of fixed financial charges to operating profit before fixed financial charges. Operating leverage is the ratio of fixed operating costs to total operating costs, usually reflecting the sensitivity of operating profit to changes in sales.

LIABILITIES—probable future sacrifices of economic benefits arising from present obligations of a particular entity to transfer assets or provide services to other entities in the future as a result of past transactions or events.

LIABILITY METHOD OF INTERPERIOD TAX ALLOCATION—an accounting method according to which the deferred tax amount reported on the balance sheet is the effect of temporary differences that will reverse in the future and that are measured using the currently enacted income-tax rates and laws that will be in existence when the temporary differences reverse. Under the liability method the deferred tax consequences of temporary differences are recognizable liabilities and assets.

LIQUIDATING DIVIDEND—a distribution out of paid-in capital usually used when a corporation permanently reduces its operations or winds up its affairs.

LIQUIDITY—the ability to pay bills when they are due. Liquidity reflects an asset's or liability's nearness to cash.

LIQUIDITY RATIOS—measures of the short-term ability of the enterprise to pay its maturing obligations and to meet unexpected cash needs.

LOSSES—decreases in equity (net assets) from peripheral or incidental transactions of an entity and from all other transactions and other events and circumstances affecting the entity during a period except those that result from expenses or distribution to owners.

LOWER-OF-COST-OR-MARKET RULE—an accounting rule that assigns the lower of the historical cost or current replacement value to an item for financial statement purposes.

MANAGEMENT—people with overall responsibility for achieving a company's goals and objectives.

MANAGEMENT ACCOUNTING—a method of accounting which provides internal users with information relating to an enterprise's resources, obligations, financial performance, budgets, and other significant operating, financing, and investing activities.

MARGIN—revenues minus specified expenses; contribution margin; gross margin.

MARGIN OF SAFETY—excess of actual or budgeted sales over break-even sales.

MARKET RATIOS—ratios that provide information and insights on the desirability of a stock investment.

MATCHING PRINCIPLE—an accounting principle that requires all expenses to be recognized in the same accounting period as the revenues with which they are associated.

MATERIALITY—an accounting assumption that requires that anything that would be of interest to an informed investor be fully disclosed in the financial statements.

MEASUREMENT—a basic accounting concept that indicates how financial information is to be reported.

MINORITY INTEREST—shareholders, or the amount of equity allocated to them, in a subsidiary that is owned partially by a parent company.

MONETARY GAIN OR LOSS—gain or loss in general purchasing power as a result of holding monetary assets or liabilities during a period when the general purchasing power of the dollar changes. During periods of inflation, holders of net monetary assets lose and holders of net monetary liabilities gain general purchasing power.

MONETARY ITEM—assets and liabilities fixed in terms of dollars by statute or contract. Cash, accounts receivable, and accounts payable are examples of monetary items.

NET ASSETS—total assets minus total liabilities; shareholders' equity.

NET INCOME—the net increase in owners' equity resulting from the profit-seeking operations of a company; revenues – expenses = net income.

NET LOSS—the excess of expenses over revenues.

NET PERIODIC PENSION EXPENSE—the pension expense recognized by a company including five elements: service cost, interest cost on projected benefit obligation, return on plan assets, amortization of unrecognized prior service cost, and gain or loss resulting from differences in actuarial assumptions and actual results.

NET PRESENT VALUE—present value of all cash inflows and outflows of a project or from a unit at a given discount rate.

NORMAL OPERATING CYCLE OF A BUSINESS—the time during which cash is used to acquire goods and services, sell the inventory (or services), and convert the sale into cash.

OBJECTIVES OF FINANCIAL REPORTING—the broad objectives of financial reporting that guide the development of accounting standards: (1) to provide information useful in investment, credit, and similar decisions, (2) to provide information useful in assessing cash flow prospects, and to provide information about enterprise resources, claims to those resources, and changes in them.

OBJECTIVITY—an accounting principle that requires the use of information that can be independently verified.

OFF-BALANCE-SHEET FINANCING—a term used to describe financing arrangements that are not reported on the face of the balance sheet, although they may be cross-referenced in the notes to the financial statements. An example is an operating lease that does not increase assets or debt; in such a case, the present value of future lease commitments for five years would be disclosed in the financial statements. Financing arrangements associated with the selling of receivables with recourse is another example of off-balance-sheet financing.

OPERATING ACTIVITIES—cash flows that include the cash impacts of transactions that are related to net income for the period; for example, collection of cash from sales, payments made to suppliers and employees, and payments made for interest, taxes, and other expenses.

OPERATING CYCLE—*See* Normal Operating Cycle of a Business.

OPERATING LEASE—a lease in which substantially all the risks and benefits of ownership have been retained by the lessor.

OPERATING LOSS CARRYFORWARD—the amount of an operating loss carryforward for tax purposes (a) reduced by the amount that offsets temporary differences that will result in net taxable amounts during the carryforward period and (b) increased by the amount of temporary differences that will result in net tax deductions for which a tax benefit has not been recognized in the financial statements.

OPPORTUNITY COST—the present value of the income (or costs) that could be earned (or saved) from using an asset in its best use alternate to the one being considered.

OWNERS' EQUITY—Assets - Liabilities = Owners' Equity. *See* Equity.

PAID-IN CAPITAL—the amount provided by owners in exchange for their investment in a corporation.

PAR VALUE—an arbitrary amount stated on a share of common or preferred stock that often signifies the legal minimum amount below which stockholders' equity cannot be reduced, except in certain circumstances.

PARENT COMPANY—a corporation that acquires over 50 percent of the voting stock of another corporation.

PARTICIPATING PREFERRED STOCK—a preferred stock that gives its holders the right to receive additional dividends along with the common stockholders.

PAYOUT RATIO (DIVIDEND YIELD)—a measure of the percentage of earnings distributed in the form of a cash dividend by dividing cash dividends by net income.

PERFORMANCE REPORTS—summaries of actual results and budgeted data.

PLANNING—establishing goals and objectives and selecting means for obtaining them.

POOLING OF INTEREST—a form of business combination in which the shareholders of the acquired corporation exchange their voting stock for that of the acquiring corporation. Twelve accounting conditions must be met before a business combination is treated as a pooling of interest.

POST-RETIREMENT BENEFIT PLANS—pension, health care services, life insurance, tuition assistance, legal and tax services, day care, housing subsidies, and other benefits provided to employees after retirement.

PREFERRED STOCK—capital stock that confers a preference to its holders over those of the common shareholders, especially preferences as to dividends and assets upon the dissolution of the corporation, but which generally lack voting rights.

PREPAID EXPENSES—assets reflecting payments for supplies or services before they are used.

PRESENT VALUE—the current value of amounts to be received or paid in the future discounted at some interest rate.

PRICE-EARNINGS RATIO—a measure of the ratio of the market price of each share of common stock to the earnings per share computed by dividing the market price of the stock by earnings per share.

PRICE INDEX—series of numbers for various periods that represent an average of prices for goods and services relative to a base period.

PRIOR PERIOD ADJUSTMENTS—items reported in the statement of retained earnings that represent material adjustments specifically identified with prior accounting periods, especially with the correction of errors of prior periods.

PROFIT CENTER—a segment of an enterprise with responsibility for controlling its own revenues and expenses to maximize its profit.

PROFIT MARGIN—the percentage of each sales dollar that results in net income; net income divided by sales.

PROFIT/VOLUME CHART—a graph showing volume on the horizontal axis and net income or sales on the vertical axis.

PROFITABILITY RATIOS—measures of the income or operating success of an enterprise for a given period of time.

PROJECTED BENEFIT OBLIGATION—the actuarial present value, at a specified date, of all the benefits attributed by the pension benefit formula to employee service rendered prior to that date. The computation involves estimates of future salary levels of employees.

PURCHASE METHOD—an accounting method used to account for a business combination in which the acquiring company issues cash or other assets, debt securities, and sometimes stock for a subsidiary's common stock.

The parent company records its investment in the subsidiary at the fair market value of the assets or securities given up or the fair market value of the common stock received, whichever is more objectively determined.

PURCHASING POWER GAIN (LOSS)—the gain (loss) that results from holding monetary liabilities (assets) during inflation or monetary assets (liabilities) during deflation.

QUALIFIED OPINION—an auditor's opinion that is given when the requirements for an unqualified opinion are not met and the auditor has limited exceptions to the client's financial statements that do not invalidate the statements as a whole. The opinion explains the reason(s) for the exception and its effect on the financial statements.

QUICK ASSETS—the sum of cash, receivables, and marketable securities.

QUICK RATIO—*See* Acid-Test Ratio.

RATE EARNED ON STOCKHOLDERS' EQUITY—a measure of profitability computed by dividing net income by total stockholders' equity.

RATE OF RETURN—the ratio of net income to the capital employed to generate that net income.

RATIO—the number resulting when one number is divided by another. Financial statement ratios are frequently used to evaluate profitability, solvency, and liquidity.

RATIO ANALYSIS—a technique of interpreting financial statements by computing financial ratios between various amounts shown on the statements. These ratios are compared with historical standards in the same company, other companies, and the industry.

REALIZATION—the process of converting noncash resources and rights into money, which usually refers to sales of assets for cash or claims to cash.

RECEIVABLE TURNOVER RATIO—a measure of the liquidity of receivables computed by dividing net credit sales by average net receivables.

RECOGNITION—the process of formally recording an item in the financial statements of an entity.

REFUNDING—the replacing of a bond issue with another bond issue.

REGULATION S-X—a major regulation of the Securities and Exchange Commission that contains the principal guidelines for accounting and reporting regulation of companies that come under its jurisdiction. This regulation specifies the form and contents of all financial statements, their notes, and schedules that are filed as part of registration statements.

RELATED PARTY TRANSACTIONS—transactions entered into between a company and its management or other parties who are responsible for making assertions in prospective financial statements. Related parties include affiliates of the enterprise; entities for which investments are accounted for by the equity method by the enterprise; trusts for the benefit of employees, such as pension and profit-sharing trusts that are managed by or under the trusteeship of management; principal owners of the enterprise; its management; members of the immediate families of principal owners of the enterprise and its management; and other parties that control or can significantly influence the management or operating policies of the other.

RELEVANCE—a quality of information that enables it to make a difference in a decision.

RELEVANT COST—a future cost that will differ among alternatives.

RELIABILITY—a quality that requires information to be reasonably free from error and bias and to represent faithfully what it purports to represent.

RESERVE—an accounting term with a variety of meanings whose use has been discouraged. The term is retained primarily to reflect the segregating of retained earnings for contingencies or other purposes.

RESPONSIBILITY ACCOUNTING—an accounting approach that establishes organizational centers for controlling revenues and costs.

RETAINED EARNINGS—that portion of total assets that came from profitable operations and that has not been distributed as a dividend.

RETURN EARNED ON COMMON STOCKHOLDERS' EQUITY—a measure of profitability computed by dividing net income, reduced by preferred dividend requirements, by common stockholders' equity.

RETURN ON ASSETS—net income divided by total assets.

RETURN ON INVESTMENT—the return per dollar of investment used to measure the efficiency with which capital resources are employed.

REVENUE—inflows or other enhancements of assets of an entity or settlements of its liabilities (or a combination of both) during a period from delivering or producing goods, rendering services, or other activities that constitute the entity's ongoing major or central operations.

REVENUE CENTER—a responsibility center that has control over revenues generated.

REVENUE REALIZATION—revenue is realized when it is earned and when an exchange has taken place. Revenue is earned when the entity has substantially accomplished what it must do to be entitled to the benefits represented by the revenues.

SECURITIES AND EXCHANGE COMMISSION—an independent, quasi-judicial agency of the U.S. government that administers and enforces the federal security laws, which include: the Securities Act of 1933, the Securities Exchange Act of 1934, Securities Investor Protection Act of 1970, the Public Utility Holding Company Act of 1935, the Trust Indenture Act of 1939, the Investment Company Act of 1940, the Investment Advisor Act of 1940, the Foreign Corrupt Practices Act of 1977, and the Insider Trading Sanctions Act of 1984. These federal securities laws seek to provide protection for investors, to ensure that securities markets are fair and honest, and, when necessary, to provide the means to enforce securities laws through sanctions. Persons aggrieved by its decisions in the exercise of its functions have a right to review by United States courts of appeals.

SEGMENT—a fairly autonomous unit or division of a company.

SIMPLE INTEREST—interest calculated on principal where interest earned during the period is not considered in the computation.

SINKING FUND—cash and other resources set aside periodically for repaying a loan or debt at maturity.

SOLVENCY—the excess of the fair market value of total assets over total liabilities.

SOLVENCY RATIOS—measures of the ability of an enterprise to survive over a long period of time.

SPECIFIC PRICE CHANGE—a change in the price of a particular good or service.

SPOT RATE—the rate of exchange of one currency for another in effect at a particular time.

STATED VALUE—an arbitrary amount assigned to no-par common stock that limits the amount that can be distributed as dividends.

STATEMENT OF CASH FLOWS—a financial report that summarizes all changes in a company's cash flows during a specified time period and its cash-related operating, investing, and financing activities.

STATEMENT OF FINANCIAL POSITION—a financial report that shows the assets, liabilities, and owners' equity of an entity at some specified time. It is commonly referred to as the **balance sheet.**

STATEMENT OF RETAINED EARNINGS—a financial report of a corporation that describes changes in the balance of retained earnings over an accounting period.

STOCK DIVIDEND—a dividend that is paid in stock in the distributing corporation.

STOCK SPLIT—an increase in the number of common shares outstanding resulting from a corresponding decrease in the par or stated value per share of common stock.

STOCKHOLDERS' EQUITY—the owners' equity of a corporation. Stockholders' equity is composed primarily of paid-in capital and retained earnings.

SUBCHAPTER S CORPORATION—a corporation with a limited number of stockholders that elects to be taxed as if it were a partnership.

SUBSEQUENT EVENTS—an event that occurs between the balance sheet date and the date of issuance of the annual report. There are two types of subsequent events that may occur: (1) ones that provide additional evidence concerning conditions that existed on the balance sheet date and (2) ones that provide evidence concerning conditions that did not exist on the balance sheet date, but instead occurred after that date but before the financial statements were issued. The first type of subsequent events require an adjustment be made to the financial statements. This type of subsequent event includes information affecting the collectability of receivables, the realization of inventories, and the settlement of liabilities. The second type of subsequent events should be disclosed in the form of a note or by other means, depending on the materiality of the financial impact. Examples of these events include a fire or flood loss, a litigation settlement, and the sale of a bond or stock issue after the balance-sheet date.

SUBSIDIARY—a corporation in which over 50 percent of the voting stock is owned by another corporation.

SUNK COST—a cost that has already been incurred and is irrelevant to the decision-making process.

TEMPORAL APPROACH—an accounting approach to translating statements from one currency to another that requires that most monetary assets and liabilities be translated at current exchange rates and most nonmonetary assets and liabilities be translated at historical exchange rates.

TEMPORARY DIFFERENCES—a difference between the tax basis of an asset or liability and its reported amount in the financial statements that will result in taxable or deductible amounts in future years when the reported amount of the asset or liability is recovered or settled, respectively. A temporary difference will result in either a tax liability that will be paid in the future or a prepaid tax that will result in a decrease in future tax payments at the then-current tax rate.

10-K—the annual report required by the SEC of most publicly held corporations.

10-Q—a quarterly report required by the SEC.

TIME VALUE OF MONEY—the concept that recognizes that payments or receipts in future time periods have less value than payments or receipts today.

TIMES INTEREST EARNED RATIO—a measure of a company's ability to meet interest payments as they come due computed by dividing income before interest expense and income taxes by interest expense.

TRADING ON THE EQUITY—*See* Leverage.

TRANSACTION—an external event involving transfer of something of value between two or more entities.

TREASURY STOCK—corporate shares reacquired by the issuing corporation for purposes other than retirement.

TROUBLED DEBT RESTRUCTURE—a situation that occurs when the creditor, for economic or legal reasons related to the debtor's financial difficulties, grants a concession to the debtor (e.g., deferment or reduction of interest or principal obligation, or modification of terms of the obligation, that it would not otherwise consider).

TURNOVER—the number of times that assets (such as inventory and accounts receivable) are replaced on the average during the period. Turnover ratios indicate how efficiently management uses its assets.

UNEARNED REVENUE—revenue not derived from normal operations or revenue received before completion of the earning process.

UNQUALIFIED OPINION—an auditor's report that is given when the auditor has formed the opinion that the statements present fairly the results of operations, financial position, and cash flows in conformance with GAAP and provide reasonable assurance that the financial statements are free of material misstatement.

VERIFIABILITY—capable of being proved by examination or investigation.

VERTICAL ANALYSIS—a method that expresses each item within a financial statement in terms of a percentage of a base amount.

VESTING—accumulated rights employees are entitled to if employment ceases.

WORKING CAPITAL—the excess of current assets over current liabilities.

YIELD—interest rate of return on a stream of cash flows.

# REFERENCES

## COMMERCIAL

Big Eight public accounting firms. Many of the Big Eight public accounting firms and regional firms publish statistics about selected industries.

Bureaus of business research at universities. Many major universities publish a wide range of regional statistics on regional industries and companies.

Dun and Bradstreet, Inc., Business Economics Division, 99 Church Street, New York, NY 10007. *Key Business Ratios* and *Cost-of-Doing Business Series.*

Financial newspapers and magazines. The *Wall Street Journal, Barron's, Forbes,* and others report current developments about companies and industries and also give in-depth reports about individual companies and industries.

Industry trade associations. Many trade associations publish financial statistics about the industry.

Investment and brokerage companies. These companies frequently track and evaluate individual companies, selected companies in an industry, or an entire industry.

Moody's Investor Service, New York, NY.

National Cash Register Company. *Expenses in Retail Businesses.*

Robert Morris Associates. *Annual Statement Studies.*

Standard & Poor's Corporation. *Industry Surveys.*

Troy, Leo. *Almanac of Business and Industrial Financial Ratios.* Prentice-Hall, Inc., Englewood Cliffs, NJ.


## *FEDERAL GOVERNMENT*

Small Business Administration.
    Small Marketers Aid.
    Small Business Management Series.
    Business Service Bulletins.

U.S. Department of Commerce. Census of Business. Wholesale Trade Report.

Department of Treasury. Statistics of Income, Corporation Income-Tax Returns. Operating Statistics.

Federal Trade Commission.

Securities and Exchange Commission.

# BIBLIOGRAPHY

## BASIC WORKS

*Accounting Trends & Techniques.* American Institute of Certified Public Accountants, New York, NY. Latest edition.

*Advances in Investment Analysis and Portfolio Management.* D. F. Reilly, editor. Jai Press, Greenwich, CT. Annual.

*Banker's Guide to Financial Statements.* T. J. O'Malia. Bank Administration Institute, Rolling Meadows, IL. 1989.

*Business Information Sources.* L. M. Daniells. University of California Press, Berkeley, CA. Latest edition.

*Business Periodicals Index.* H. W. Wilson, Bronx, NY. Monthly.

*C.F.A. Readings in Financial Analysis.* Association for Investment Management and Research, Charlottesville, VA. Latest edition.

*Corporate Financial Analysis.* D. R. Harrington and B. D. Wilson. Business One Irwin, Homewood, IL.

*Directory of Business and Financial Services.* M. McNierney Grant and R. Berleant-Schiller. Special Libraries Association. Latest edition.

*Financial Statement Analysis.* G. Foster. John Wiley & Sons, New York, NY.

*Guide to Statistical Sources in Money, Banking, and Finance.* M. Balachandran. Oryx Press, Phoenix, AZ. 1988.

*Information Sources in Finance and Banking.* R. G. Lester and J. Cropley, editors. R. R. Bowker, New Providence, NJ. 1991.

*Investments: An Introduction to Analysis and Management.* W. F. Sharpe and G. J. Alexander. Prentice-Hall, Englewood Cliffs, NJ. Latest edition.

*Modern Portfolio Theory and Investment Analysis.* E. J. Elton and M. J. Gruber. John Wiley & Sons, New York, NY.

*Security Analysis: Principles and Techniques.* B. Graham and S. Cottle. McGraw-Hill, New York, NY. Latest edition.

*Standard and Poor's Industry Surveys.* Standard and Poor's Corp., New York, NY. Looseleaf service.

## BOOKS AND MANUALS

*Analysis of Financial Statements.* L. A. Bernstein. Business One Irwin, Homewood, IL. Latest edition.

*Analyst's Handbook: Composite Corporate Per Data.* Standard and Poor's Corp., New York, NY. Annual.

*Corporate Financial Analysis.* D. R. Harrington and I. D. Wilson. Business One Irwin, Homewood, IL. Latest edition.

*Encyclopedia of Banking and Finance.* C. J. Woelfel. Bank Administration Institute, Rolling Meadows, IL. Ninth edition.

*Financial Analysts Handbook.* S. N. Levine. Business One Irwin, Homewood, IL. Latest edition.

*Financial Statement Analysis: A Practitioner's Guide.* M. Fridson. John Wiley & Sons, Inc., New York, NY.

*Financial Statement Analysis: The Basics and Beyond.* R. M. Bukics. Probus, Chicago, IL. 1991.

*Fraud, Window Dressing and Negligence in Financial Statements.* I. Kellogg. Shepard's McGraw-Hill, Colorado Springs, CO. Looseleaf service.

*How to Analyze Business, Financial Statements & the Quality of Earnings.* J. G. Siegel. Prentice-Hall, Englewood Cliffs, NJ.

*How to Interpret Financial Statements for Better Business Decisions.* B. E. Miller and D. E. Miller. AMACOM, New York, NY. 1990.

*The Numbers You Need.* N. J. Hopkins and others, editors. Gale Research Inc., Detroit, MI. 1992.

*Quantitative Analysis for Financial Analysis.* S. J. Brown and M. P. Kritzman, editors. Business One Irwin, Homewood, IL. 1990.

*Reading and Interpreting Financial Statements.* American Management Association Extension Institute, Saranac Lake, NY. Looseleaf service.

*Techniques of Financial Analysis.* E. A. Helfert. Irwin, Homewood, IL. Latest edition.

*Understanding Financial Statements.* G. Gordon. South-Western, Cincinnati, OH. 1991.

*Winning Numbers: How to Use Business Facts and Figures to Make Your Point and Get Ahead.* M. C. Thomsett. AMACOM, American Management Association. New York, NY. 1990.

*Worldwide Financial Reporting & Audit Requirements.* Peat Marwick International Staff. Peat Marwick, Chicago, IL.

## *ONLINE DATABASES*

*Compustat.* Standard and Poor's. Englewood, CO.

*Disclosure Database.* Disclosure, Inc. Bethesda, MD.

*Dunsprint.* Dun and Bradstreet, Murray Hill, NJ.

*Inves Text.* Thomas Financial Services, Boston, MA.

*NAARS.* American Institute of Certified Public Accountants. National Automated Accounting Research System, New York, NY.

# INDEX

# ABOUT THE AUTHOR

Charles J. Woelfel, Ph.D, CPA has authored numerous books and professional and academic journal articles in business, finance, law, accounting and professional ethics. His most recent book is *The Handbook of Bank Accounting*. He is also the Editor of the ninth and tenth editions of *Encyclopedia of Banking and Finance*. Currently a Professor of Accounting at the University of North Carolina at Greensboro, Woelfel received his undergraduate degree from Notre Dame University, a master's degree from Butler University, a doctorate from the University of Texas at Austin, and a diploma from the Southwestern Graduate School of Banking at Southern Methodist University.